To My Sister Courtney

Thank u so much 4 your support

Looking For LOVE 'N ALL THE WRONG FACES

Lasting Love or... lust, lies and losses

by
Ms Cynthia

authorHOUSE®

AuthorHouse™
1663 Liberty Drive, Suite 200
Bloomington, IN 47403
www.authorhouse.com
Phone: 1-800-839-8640

© 2008 Ms Cynthia. All rights reserved.

No part of this book may be reproduced, stored in a retrieval system, or transmitted by any means without the written permission of the author.

First published by AuthorHouse 5/12/2008

ISBN: 978-1-4343-5367-2 (sc)

Printed in the United States of America
Bloomington, Indiana

This book is printed on acid-free paper.

This book is dedicated to Joyce Anderson-Elmore

This dedication is to a woman who has indeed been a blessing in my life. She continues to be an inspiration and one that I am elated to call my friend.

Our first meeting was the result of a business recommendation from a common acquaintance, Daniel Hawkins. He knew she would appreciate the artwork I sold. After speaking at length, we realized how many common interests we shared - African art, plays, dining, books and jazz music just to name a few. We also had a deep appreciation for God's initial creations; beautiful places of peace and tranquility. Those places and sites which showcased tall trees, botanical gardens, rippling lakes, slow flowing rivers and sparkling waterfalls. We talked extensively on long walks on winding trails and just sat quietly while viewing amazing sunsets or moon and starlit evenings. Many of the places we indulged were with her daughter Charity that is hearing/speech impaired. Her mother understood the importance of exposing her to all the beauty this world offers and to appreciate the faculties she's been blessed with; enjoying them to the fullest. I am thankful to have witnessed this mother's love and to have shared in those experiences. As I continued to pursue my other interest, including writing, I was quite influenced, encouraged and inspired by the two of them.

Our lives continue to unfold revealing many faces, phases, projects, surprises, hugs, disappointments, tears, dinners, shoes, cocktails, trips, walks, candles, long night talks, scares, laughter, calls of concern, encouragement and thoughtful gestures on both our part. Surprisingly, neither of us enjoy talking on the phone – only when necessary – go figure.

For that, and so much more, I thank you Joyce and proudly dedicate this labor of love from me to you. I love and appreciate you and your family for your support. You've been my ace girl.

Always with Love,
Cynthia

To My Business Manager, Napoleon Curtain

Well **Napoleon**, where do I begin? I know saying "thank you" from the heart is suppose to be sufficient in most cases, but I also know for sure, that in this case, it cannot begin to express my deep and sincere appreciation for the conscientiousness you've exhibited.

I'm sure when you signed on to be my business manager you envisioned a new venture, a way to capitalize on that business degree, a way to 'be the man'. Ha, did you ever get what you wished for. This year has brought you to task in a way, I'm sure, you never expected – I know I didn't.

You were faced with obstacles that neither of us could have expected, but you dug in and got it done. When the doors were closed, you knocked. When they didn't answer, did you rip the doors off? How'd you do that? I know - prayer.

Well at least now you're knowledgeable of the business side of the literary game. I say game because so many were played. You made wise choices when to play and when not to. And just think, now you are a great camera man, cashier, bodyguard, scheduler, book seller, driver (don't mention the gas), set-up guy, cold calls phone solicitor, book hauler and the like. Who would 'a thought you'd amount to so much because of a little book that came into your life.

But seriously, it is my prayer that we will be rewarded greatly for all our hard work and dedication. Your focus and persistence has kept me going when I really wanted to give up. Because of your belief in my ability to break into this complex field, I couldn't let you or our faithful customers down and thus – here we go again, book two and Cd one **Looking for Love 'n All the Wrong Faces**

Thank your mom, **Mrs. Irene,** for her story of love. Thank **Gwen** for going to sleep while she was suppose to be helping me get the story - I tell you. Kidding, I really appreciated the Pawley's Island help – man, it was hott!

Nap, our customers, friends and even relatives have really kept us both encouraged. That speaks volumes about the way they feel toward you. You've been so committed they feel comfortable climbing aboard this roller coaster ride. Now prove us right - Put this thing in gear and let's head onward and upward!

Wes, I'm excited about our collaboration. Your **jazz** definitely compliments my written words! **"Love, Lies & Hanky Panky"** is an effort I'm proud to place my name and reputation on. Yes!

Great job everyone. Keep up the good work! Now, enough of this jaw jacking – get back to work – we've got books to sell, books to sign-shows to do – yeah, yeah, the check is in the mail, whatever. What gas money??? Ge-ee-ze

With Sincere Thanks, Appreciation and much Love - Cynthia

I sincerely thank you for your support, and I hope you enjoy my particular style of creative writing. More important, I pray that this book informs, encourages, motivates and touches your life in a thought-provoking yet heartwarming way!

I welcome and encourage your comments at
tomscynthia@gmail.com

Always With Love,
Ms Cynthia

Acknowledgements

To My Children: **LaCherri, Jarrard, and Elgin**
I take this opportunity to thank you for your love and support through the years.

So often, people ask, "How do you manage to do so many things?" "You're always trying new ventures, projects and businesses, how do you do it?"

I can only smile and say "God blessed me with great kids. They are self-sufficient and they encourage their mother to "go for it!" They've been able to skirt around trouble as best they could, which allowed my spirit the freedom to fly. Though I'm sure my children have had, and continue to have needs, they've somehow managed to work it out without placing a burden on mom. They support me, or to be honest, tolerate me, and I 'm just blessed to know them and have such respectful beings as my children".
Kids, for that – THANK YOU and THANK **GOD** FOR YOU!

Anbriel, I thank you for being the sweetest god-daughter ever!
I thank you **Joy, James, Lisa, Robin and Sharika.** Welcome to our world. Thank you guys for taking good care of our little ones – my grand kids - **Jahkim, Camron, Makayla, Kingston, Korey, Sierra, E.J., Jordan and Kendall.**

Mary, you and your mom **Mary** (another Mary, Mary) did a great job with your kids. **Antron and Tasha** I thank you both for your

respect, support and loyalty through the years. It proves that love overrides bloodline. We secured our bond during that summer in Atlanta years ago, it seems like only yesterday. Know that your children are also precious to me – **Maya, Antron** (Budda), **Daibrelle,** and your new arrival, little **Prince Uriah** – **Congrats Trice**
I Love you all this-----------------------------------much!!! Kisses

Cherie George, I continue to thank **God** for the day we met and I was introduced to that little cottage on the lake – such an inspiration for creating and a peaceful respite for me. I am so thankful for that little piece of paradise.

Karen and Dave, I couldn't have asked for neighbors as kind and thoughtful as the two of you. One of the beauties of the lake experience has been having you guys as neighbors. Sh-h-h-h, this secret hide-a-way is some-kind'a special huh? Thanks guys for the love and support you've extended.

JESUS LOVES ME
– THIS I KNOW –
EVERYDAY HE SHOWS ME SO

Authors note

"**To My Sisters**" story books were created to inspire grown women to remember a time in our early lives when pretty pictures told pretty stories and all dreams were said to come true. To be a girl was to live and love. Romance was the ultimate life goal. Joy and fulfillment was understood, and we would all live and thrive happily ever after – ha, what a joke.

After reflecting briefly on those lies, you can read about our real life stories in the same rhythmic tone, and appreciate why we were never told the truth. After all, what would a girl have to look forward to? The beautiful thing is – we can decide to live 'happily ever after' after all.

These stories of reality are written in lyrics and short story format, displaying various font styles, giving each woman's circumstance it's own voice. It is written for easy reading, makes a quick point for the busy working woman, and helps us laugh at ourselves and our friends. The stories are written in a way that helps us be more patient with those sisters that just don't get it yet. Throughout the book are also overall wellness suggestions from head to toe, and everything in between, yes, literally.

So girls, I personally invite you to get that cup of warm tea, glass of wine, box of chocolates, whatever your indulgence, and prepare to laugh, cry, think, feel encouraged and be proud that **God** created you female – a woman with beauty and strength to overcome, and the ability to endure it all in the name of Love - Love for self. I thank each of you dearly for your support.

The good news, the guys are reading these books and are getting it. Their responses and comments to me are very encouraging. Thank you especially to **Mike Cureton, Claude Smith Jr.** for your loving support through the years! Special thanks to **Otis Thomas (Power Poet)** for your **'Paradigm Concepts'**.
And to all you guys that made purchases – thanks.
U know I 'preciate it!

Ms Cynthia

Please see comments and pictures from previous book readings and signings located on the back pages. Included are pictures from our first book's release party **"THE BOOK EXPLOSION"** held at the **Ballroom** in **Greenville, SC** owner **John Lewis**, hosted by **Judy Thompson** and friends

Once upon a time…

MS Cynthia

…GOD LOOKED AT HIS WORK AND SAW THAT IT WAS GOOD. HE THEN CREATED MAN AND CALLED HIM 'ADAM'. AFTER LOOKING AT MAN ADAM, GOD SOON REALIZED SOME IMPROVEMENT WOULD BE NECESSARY. HE THEN PLACED MAN 'ADAM' UNDER A DEEP SLEEP, AND THE ART OF BEAUTY, BRAINS AND MAGNIFICENCE BEGAN.

IT TOOK HIM MANY HOURS TO ARRIVE AT THIS WONDERFUL CREATION, BUT AFTER OBSERVING HER, HE KNEW SHE WAS WELL WORTH ALL THE HARD WORK HE'D PUT IN – ABSOLUTELY!

"AWAKE ADAM! I HAVE MADE SOMEONE VERY SPECIAL FOR YOU. THIS SHOULD PROVE THE EXTENT OF MY LOVE FOR YOU. AWAKE ADAM, SHE IS INDEED AWESOME. I HAVE TO ADMIT – I OUT-DID MYSELF. WE MUST GIVE HER A DESERVING NAME. WHAT SHALL WE CALL HER?"

ADAM AWOKE AND COULDN'T BELIEVE HIS EYES. HE SHOUTED IN AMAZEMENT
"OH MY GOD"
GOD SAID "NO ADAM, THAT'S MY NAME REMEMBER?"

ADAM STILL ASTONISHED THAT SHE WAS FOR HIM AND HIM ALONE EXCLAIMED
"WHOA!" "MAN!"

AND THE CREATOR SAID "AS YOU WISH ADAM, SHE SHALL BE CALLED "WOMAN", NOW GO INTRODUCE YOURSELF.

MAN ADAM, BESIDE HIMSELF, SPOKE TO HIS QUEEN. HIS WORDS STUMBLING, HE SPOKE "GOOD EVE WHOA MAN

THE BEGINNING...

Contents

MY DEAR HEAVENLY FATHER, ... 1
WAKE UP SISTER, WE'RE WAITING FOR YOU 3
MY SISTERS FLOW LIKE JAZZ 5

LOVING LIES & HANKY PANKY

LOOKING FOR LOVE IN ALL THE WRONG FACES 11
WHAT HE DOESN'T KNOW -WON'T HURT YOU 13
IT'S WHAT HE'S NOT SAYING 15
FAILING CHEMISTRY 19
FORGET ME NOT 21
I JUST KNEW HE WAS THE ONE 23
FRIEND GIRLS NON INVASIVE PROCEDURES 25
PRISON LOVER 27
OH BABY, I'M GONN'A LOVE YOU RIGHT! 29
RUFUS EARL 32
SLEEPING WITH PETE 34
BUSINESS MATTERS 36
VIDEO DIVA/SHAKE DANCE QUEEN 38

Domestic & Social ILLS

WHAT'S WRONG WITH THAT GIRL? 47
WHO'S UNCLE JOHN AND AUNT IVA? 50

AND THE BEAT GOES ON	54
THE COLOR WAS RED	57
A BAD CASE OF THE A'LEASE-HE	59
MRS SOMEBODY III	61
MOMMY HE HURTS ME	64
CAUSE OF DEATH – A BROKEN HEART	66
HIV/AIDS	74
KEEP YOUR HANDS TO YOURSELF	76
FEATURE - CRACK JONES, BAD TO THE BONE	77

BLESSINGS AFFIRMATIONS ENCOURAGEMENT

BLINDED BY THE LIGHT	89
THANK GOD FOR COVERAGE	91
LORD, WHERE'S MY CHILD	93
PRAY IT ALL AWAY	95
SPIRITUAL HEALINGS	97

TO MY SPOKEN WORD SISTERS & BROTHERS

MY BOOK IN MY HAND	101
WHITE DARKNESS	103
WORDS	105
IS SEEING OR FEELING BELIEVING?	110

FOR MEN ONLY

FOR MEN ONLY	115
METHODOLOGY FOR GREAT HANKY PANKY	117
THE MEN WHO LOVE US	122

SISTER STRENGTH

PEARLS FOR MY GIRLS	129

YOU LOVE ME? I CAN'T TELL 133
THE LOVE YOURSELF CHALLENGE 135
MRS. IRENE – SHE LIVES NEXT DOOR TO HERSELF... 136
FIFTY/50 LOVE 139
OH NOTHIN' HONEY, JUST TALKIN TO MYSELF 142
YOUNG GIRLS ADMIRATION **144**

THE SWEETEST THING THAT NEVER HAPPENED

THE SWEETEST THING THAT *NEVER* HAPPENED....149

LOVING US FIT FOR US WOE IS US

I'VE ONLY HAD SALAD! 163
THE HAIR DOWN THERE 166
IS THE GYNO A GIGOLO 168
JUST US GIRLS- FEMALE ANATOMY 171
GOOD BYE TO PIES STAY AWAY FAT THIGHS 177
THAT'S THE LAST WORD – PERIOD! 180
FROM PAMPERS TO DEPENDS DRIP, DRIP, DRIP 182
FRIEND GIRLS RECIPE 184
SOUTHERN SWEETNESS **186**
PURE SOUTHERN HOSPITALITY 188
GETTIN FIT **190**
FREE YOUR GIRLS! 193
LEFTY'S STORY 195

WE GIRLS & OUR ISSUES

DAMAGED GOODS 201
YES! I SHOP 'TIL I DROP 203
PUT IT ON MY CARD 205
NO MORE ROOM IN MY MENTAL WOMB 207

THE MALL IS EVIL 208
WHAT DA'YA MEAN WE'RE BREAKIN UP? 210
STILL SASSY AND SEXY AT SEVENTY 212
WHERE, OH WHERE ARE THE REAL MEN? 214
FEMALE VANITY STAGES 216

PICTURES AND SHARED THOUGHTS FROM MY READERS
ABOUT THE AUTHOR 227

My Dear heavenly father,

Hey lord, it's me again
Asking for help and strength again,
Knowing I need you before I begin
The one, on whom, I can truly depend

I thank you for my last published book,
It was a good start; it was a great hook,
Your love and guidance was all it took
They loved the cover, they liked that look

Well, like I said, I need your hand
Something the ladies will understand,
Something they'll even demand,
Something sweet, something grand!

A little something to make them smile,
Soothing, calming, help them relax awhile,
As they laugh, blush and giggle like a child,
Armored with strength as we strut and style
Marching in harmony on this uphill mile

Allow me the words we've been ashamed to say
a whimsical, yet respectful way
keep it really real and truly true
adult women blessed with beauty and passion too
Help them understand; these blessings come from you

Before i begin, I give you praise
I'll give you praise for the rest of my days
thank you for this opportunity
And for allowing me to be "Still Just Me"
I pray for your continued grace and mercy

With love- once again,

    Amen
                Cynthia

Wake up Sister, We're Waiting for You

Ms Cynthia

Sister you've slept far too long
Wake up; it's time to get up
You've slept through the alarms
You've slept through the coaxing
Wake up girl, please wake up
We're waiting for you, time to get up

You've slept through the nightmares
Wake up from those tears
Sister, don't just turn away
Wake up, face your fears

You remain fast asleep
avoiding another day
But every day, my sister
is another day
Wake up

A new day awaits you
Waiting with open arms
Open arms filled with love
Secure, strong and warm
Girl, get up

We too were once asleep
Afraid to open, afraid to peep
Danger lurking everywhere
Troubled; no one seemed to care
But try it; it's a brand new day
We've learned to love a better way
Wake up

No more dreams of falling and failing
No more bottomless pits
We're waiting here to catch you
We'll help mend the pieces every bit
Come, live your life, get up

Come sister, face your final cloud
It's filled with gentle rain
Scream girl, thunder loud!
Unleash the anxiety, release the pain
You're a queen, come claim your reign!

A sleeping beauty awake again
Saved by Grace in Jesus name, amen

Now breathe girl; a deep cleansing breath. Now smile a big smile
Feel the warmth and bask in the sunlight - thank God for that warm hug!
Now walk into your new day – your new life, knowing that you're loved
Sister, we're so thankful you're awake
We missed you, need you and we love you

Welcome back girl !

MY SISTERS FLOW LIKE JAZZ

Ms Cynthia

Can you hear them? The tapping sounds of jazz
Walking in stiletto heals in sync
Strolling through the street; a funky beat
Long, strutting strides, the rhythm of their feet,
Stepping and flowing like Jazz

Colors of cobalt blue, emerald green and teal
Fire engine red and platinum grays of steel
Yam colors; a down-home meal
Garments of silk, linen and cotton blend
Their stride; simply flawless - perfect Zen
Yes, these ladies are hot, sweet and spicy
Smothered in cayenne Cajun sauce
Sprinkled with granules of pure sugar- in the raw
Dancing and flowing like sweet fiery Salsa Jazz

Sisters hot and bakery fresh like out of the oven
They have risen to the occasion dressed to the nines
Musical laughter; melodic ring tone
Tingles to the core, straight to the bone
Swinging their hair like sounds from
A trombone playing awesome, sexy Jazz

Flavored lips, colored nails and cheeks
Burst of shades borrowed from the evening sun
Amber, rusty brick and toasted golden orange
Hair shades of sinful red, chocolate brown,

raven black and corn silk yellow, platinum crowns
All in various forms like Calypso Jazz

Soft locks, short sassy cuts
Curls, spirals, kinks and braids
And one drew envy from the ocean
a long flowing finger wave
The ocean was jealous - for this hair
 Swayed like a tidal wave of new wave Jazz

They smelled of jasmine, rosé petals, ying and yang
Citrus and spice, pineapple lemon meringue
Coconut, tangerine and essence of kiwi
 Earth smells of a steaming cup of green tea
Pleasurable aromas to smell, hear, and see
Like flavors and scents of Sophisticated Jazz

As they strolled you could hear the sax
There was razz m' tazz and all that jazz
Uniquely different from fusion jazz
Men's heads swelling like contusion jazz
Nothing about this was confusion jazz
The composition was complex
 They threw their long pearls around their necks
Like big band blazing sounds of Jazz

Sisters understanding our common link
Smiling and gliding; an ice rink
Glancing up into a Juniper sky
Their reflection from the hot ice

Diamonds, rubies, sapphires
Rare jewels and fragrant flowers
flowed to their melody, all in harmony
Like Contemporary Jazz

Sparkling bracelets, bangles and earrings
Brilliantly bouncing off the dance floor
Glittering, shimmering jewelry galore
Lightening bolts igniting shock waves
The electrifying cymbals and chimes play
Like syncopated, embellished Swing Jazz

Polka dots, stripes and shocking shades of pink
Floral sundresses – sun caresses, lashes blink
Their butts; the bass, their breast; the drums
Squee-bop. Bee-bop, Squi- dily- doo
Sisters flowing like classy sisters do

Visual rhapsody for the imagination to see
Sisters free styling; being all they can be
Replicating a zesty Cuban rumba
Imagine - sight, smell and taste; a Brazilian samba
Emotional, blistering, scorching, searing, sizzling moves
They are life's jazzy sisters 'cause they flow to a groove
It's like, it's like, it's like – what else?

Like Jazz-z-z-z-z-

LOVING LIES & HANKY PANKY

Looking for Love in all the Wrong Faces

MS CYNTHIA

I'm so lonesome. I could use a good strong hug right about now
A kiss would be nice, hell, just some company
Why is love so hard to find these days?
Let me call him again. Darn, the answering machine again
*"Hello, this is me again. I was waiting for you to call me back
This is the fifth message so I guess you're not home yet.
OK, I'll try you a little later. Give me a call ok? Bye"*
I was going to fix dinner and everything; he won't even call me back
"Mommy, can I come in and show you my picture I drew of you"?
No, not now, I'm busy on the phone!
"Mommy, we're hungry"
I'm not cooking; eat a pop tart or something. I'm resting
Let me try Eva
*"Hey girl, what'ya doing? Oh, you are? OK, I'll call you tomorrow
or call me back when you finish. I really need to talk girl".*
"Mommy, can we come in and watch TV with you"?
No! I really wish you kids would leave me alone. I'm busy!
Surely, Theresa is home; she's laid off
*"Hello, hey girl you want to get something to eat and maybe
hit a bar or two? I'm buying. Oh really? Yeah, some other time
I know it's the last minute. Call me sometime".*
"Hey mama, I got an 'A' on my project. Want' a see?

Look! I told you kids to leave me alone. I'm depressed and I
don't want to be aggravated. Everybody's too damned busy
to spend any time with me. They all have their lives. OK, fine!
What about me? Who do I have? Huh? Who wants to love me?

*Girlfriend, there is no love greater than God's love, and the
next best thing is the love from your children. The love they
offer is so sweet, so forgiving, so real. There is no man or friend
that will love you more or offer such an unconditional love than
those little people in your life, knocking at your door waiting
to pour all the dirty, sticky, juicy, wet loving on you that you can
stand. A love that surpasses anything that you're begging for
from that man. Give 'em a hug and feel what true love is all about.
It will be appreciated and reciprocated just like love is suppose to be.*

What He Doesn't Know -Won't Hurt You

Ms Cynthia

No! Please don't make that mistake
Letting him know how much you will take
Opening your past, letting him see
how vulnerable you've allowed yourself to be

Total honesty - is not - telling it all
You'll sit wondering why he doesn't call
Listen-up girls, I'm telling ya'll

He'll store those secrets 'til you least suspect
Then pull them out to show you disrespect
Hanging each tale you told around your neck

You'll stand there crying
"How could you do this to me?
Said you'd never bring this up,
didn't we agree?
I thought you wanted total honesty!"

He'll smile then frown, that's what he'll do
Then tell you he's repulsed by you
Who's to blame that you shared so much?
You told this, that, such and such
Now you wonder "where's the soft sweet touch"?

Once again you'll cry
"All men are the same"
Perhaps you'll learn one day
Stop playing the Tell It All Game

IT'S WHAT HE'S NOT SAYING
Listen between the lines

ten by Ms Cynthia

OK girl, I've gotta go, he's here. No, just conversation tonight, you know, get to know each other better, see where he's coming from. Yeah girl, I'll call you -bye.

"Hi, welcome to my home, glad you could make it" (*Damn, he sure is gorgeous and fi-i-i-ine!*)

"Hey, I'm glad I made it too, thanks for having me over". (*Yeah boy, this is just right for a playa' like me to lay and play all day. Big screen, surround sound system, oh yes!*"

"So, can I get you something? I prepared some appetizers, would you care for a cocktail"? (*OK, he didn't bring flowers, candy or wine. Oh well, he doesn't really know me or what I like so I'll let it slide this time*).

"Yes, thank you, some cognac would be nice. I really enjoy the burn." (*She's got a nice well stocked bar, me and my boyz are going to ball out!*)

"Sure, I have some right here. Would you like Martel, Remy or Hennessy?" (*Hell, you don't like the burn that well; you didn't bring a damn thing*)

"Here you are. Now tell me about yourself. Who am I dealing with here?
(*All the chick mags say we shouldn't talk so much, allow him to share*)

"Oh, you know, I'm just me. A man trying to take a stand, understand? You know a playa trying to make a dollar out of fifteen cents, you know".

(*Is this fool a played out rapper or what?*)

"Well, really I don't know. Tell me more. What interest do you have? What do you do, I mean, for a living?

"Well, I'm actually self-employed, an entrepreneur, you know. But because of this economy I'm a little financially embarrassed right now. But hey, I've got some big plans for future endeavors. (*That should hold her for right now. She asks too many damn questions*)

Oh really, like what if you don't mind me asking. I'm interested in you. I don't want to get all in your business but just share a little and then I'll tell you some things about me and my interest. (*Tell me something other than your need for the burn. It's obvious he's out of work, but then, the economy is bad. I'm being judgmental, let me stop*)

"Well, you know I like hanging out with my boyz politicking and bull-shiting and conver-sating, you know, this, that there and the other. I also look out for my mom a lot cause, you know, you owe that to your mom. So I spend a lot of time looking after her."

"Oh, is she disabled"?

"Nawh, she's just my rock, you know. I look out for her place while she's working. (*Man, she's nosy!*)

"I see, you live with your mom while you're between job, I mean career, business dealings?" (*Oh hell, what kind of 'cheese is these' I'm dealing with?*)

"Yeah, that's it, you're on point! But see, it works for both of us. She really hates being alone and she needs me there to have male presence. You know, to keep the undesirables away. But look here baby, as soon as I'm on my feet, I'm going to be looking for someone just like you. (*Fine, good job, independent, pretty, well not so much, but PAID!*) And I'll be ready to get married and start a family and be the man my pops never was. (*Hope she don't find out I've already got four kids and some ass-kicking child support payments, which I'm going to pay my mama back*) So come on over here girl and let's really get to know each other better"

After appetizers, a few drinks, some relaxing music, which he really seemed to enjoy, we chilled, yeah, even he chilled...

"OK, I'm hearing you and I'm feeling you, let's get closer".

He's thinking: "Man, I had to do some major rapping to this honey, but I think I'm set. I'm going to hit this real good and hell, I'll be moving in by next week".
She's thinking:

"Yeah player, I know what you're thinking, but I'm horney and feeling real sexy. I want to get my freak on and you are fine as that last glass of wine. You're not hitting this, I'm hitting that, and I'm going to get my cognac's worth out of your ass. The player is getting played tonight. Let's see, where's my condoms? Ah yes, he did bring something and I like it, actually I could love this piece! Baby you may not be employed, but trust me, you're going to work tonight! OK, ok I've got to stay focused. I might let him stay the night if it's as good as it looks, but first thing in the morning he needs to get his ass on to his mama. He probably needs to drive her to work; that's probably her car. Anyway and whatever, I'm not letting this player get any sleep tonight, hell, he doesn't work, he can sleep all day at his mama's house. **"Play on Play-ette!"**

FAILING CHEMISTRY

MS CYNTHIA

Vaguely remember you
we met- we became
me you 2

couldn't wait to hear your voice
waited anyway – no choice

Loved your smell
smell turned stale
love whispers turned 2 yells
piece of heaven - now hell

Kisses – glucose erased
desperate to win this race
no more - all a waste
Your x'es, my y's?
U answer my y's with a lie

DNA no longer mix
gotta break out'ta this shit

Test score - **Very low**
A do over?
Far 2 many mistakes
was this our best?
If so, we failed this test
There's no more chemistry

The Na $H2O$ *pouring from the wells of my eyes*
will only rust your Fe *heart*
I must leave, I must breathe; I need O
enough boo-hoo's filled with CO_2

FORGET ME NOT

Ms Cynthia

My dear, my baby as we part
Baby please, keep my heart
Our love solid; truly real
Happiness, lust, total zeal
Please forget me not

My love's committed and it's true
This love is blessed for me and you
Our love will stand near or far
However no matter where we are
Forget me not

Please my love, understand
No matter what, you're still my man
Baby, on that, you can stand
Come baby, give me your hand
Forget me not

No sad good byes, no need to cry
Look in my eye, you're still my guy
Don't look sadly asking why
Just remember - forget me not

I need you so, never let me go
Don't say no. No, baby no
Oh well, if you say so

Baby, you knew I had to go
Please forget me not

Sorry baby, this hurts so
Really gotta go, you know?
Another day, another row to hoe
You're forever in my heart though

Guessed we'd be together; tie the knot
That's what I get for guessing; I guess not
Tired of begging; offered a lot
Let's cross the 't'; for the 'i' a dot
No putting me on the spot
I'll forget you! …Not

I Just Knew He Was the One

Ms Cynthia

OK, one night I was partying, you know, having fun
Some dude ask me, at the end of the night, if I'd like to make a run
We hung out, got some food, well; you know… then the sun
I called, beeped, looked for him 'cause I'm pregnant with his son

Then I met this clean cut guy; so sweet and nice!
I cleaned, washed and ironed his clothes, even made beans and rice
He was loving, kept me laughing, gave me thrills and chills
I just knew he was the one, of course, I got off my pills
Pregnant again, he was long gone, I sat there looking ill

I'd surely learned my lesson; at least that's what I thought
I knew all the pitfalls, so sure I wouldn't get caught
Now with my boyfriends, I had condoms and/or creams
But one guy brought over a friend, they pulled a tag team
Abused, not knowing what to do, I asked myself "is this my fault too?"
Another child, I don't have a clue, which one is your dad Little Pooh

So there I was, sad again, three kids and no man
Met this hard working dude, he wanted to lend a hand
A giving type of guy; good to my three kids
People you won't believe this, the messed up crap I did

I cheated on this good man for a sorry piece of crap
No money for a hotel room, I made love in his car in his lap
My good man rode up on us, he went home and calmly moved out
A few weeks later, missed my period, hell yeah, I crapped out!

I'm a single mom with four kids; I'm always feeling sad
I sit here reflecting on the many chances I've had
Not that I feel sorry for me; for my kids I feel bad
They deserve better answers than I give for -
"Hey mama, who and where is my dad?"

FRIEND GIRLS NON INVASIVE PROCEDURES

MS CYNTHIA

Use these procedures liberally as needed for mild mental blowouts and those painful matters of the heart. If conditions last longer than you, as a friend, find acceptable, immediately seek professional help.
Good Luck!

Apply pressure around the upper arms and shoulder area with a big hug while gently patting the back area.

Allow tears to flow freely. Whisper softly "Its ok girl, let it go, I'm here for you."

Nose area will drain heavily. Have an adequate supply of tissues readily available.

A cool white face cloth is often very soothing to the forehead and eye area. (Limit colored ones: no dyes in the eyes)

After a while, back away from the hugs and hold a hand softly while listening attentively. Keep questions to a minimum and voice tone low. Do not make any negative comments-absolutely none.(No, especially not the one about him and how you told her so).

There will be bruised feelings, often abrasive language and very often a bleeding heart. These are all natural occurrences for breakups and discoveries of underhanded behavior.

After the temperament has stabilized, you may offer to stay with her, offer to take the kids off her hands for a few hours or perhaps overnight, offer to make her a warm cup of caffeine free or herbal tea. Ask if she'd like for you to turn off the ringer on her phone, she can still check her messages if she chooses to. Upon leaving, suggest she take a warm shower or an aromatherapy bubble bath (never hot, too stimulating). Suggest a soft pair of pajamas. If she insists on a glass of wine – indulge her – you probably can use one as well. One glass should help her sleep better, two or more will probably reverse all you've accomplished. Keep tissues handy.

Surprise her, the day after, with a gift bag filled with scented candles, herbal teas, a soft cute sleep set, a jazz CD (she doesn't need worded music right now), and books that are affirming, creative and encouraging. A couple of recommendations: **To My Sisters with Love** and **Looking for Love 'n all the Wrong Faces**, just to name two I'm familiar with. I believe they're both authored by Ms Cynthia.

Love her, listen to her and let her talk herself through her dilemma. She'll be ever so grateful to have you as her friend. *A friend girl in need; needs a girlfriend indeed.*

In cases of physical or sexual abuse
SEEK LAW ENFORCEMENT AND MEDICAL ATTENTION FIRST!

PRISON LOVER

Ms Cynthia

The sweetest love letters galore, every day
The sweetest poems and poetry – too beautiful to read
Phone calls – sugary sweet
        Then…
Where ya' at? What ya' doing?, Where ya' going?
Elongated new dictionary vocabulary
Newly learned legal jargon
More beautiful love letters
Phone calls – precious & sweet
        Then…
Where were ya when I called?
What time ya' getting here?
What ya' bring me?
Why ya' leaving so soon?
        Then…
Beautiful quoted Biblical scriptures
More beautifully written love letters
Letters to be forwarded to a new attorney
        Then…
I'm gonna make this all up to you one day
I'm gonna be the man you need some day
I'm gonna get out of this place soon
We're going on the best honeymoon
        Then…

Can ya' call this person for me?
Can ya' call that person for me?
When did ya' call? What time?
Did ya' say what I told you? What'd they say?
Ask 'em if I can call them!
>> Then...
More beautifully written letters
More passionate phone calls
I'm gonna make it up to you
Baby, thanks for waiting for me
>> Then...
You think you can sign for me a business loan?
Can you go get me a …
Can you pick me up a …
You tired of waiting for me?
Don't come back to see me
Where you been girl? Don't you know I love you girl?
How much change you got on ya? Leave it on my book
They cut out love-making visits – I wanna do you girl!

Oh Baby, I'm gonn'a Love You Right!

Ms Cynthia

Oh baby, I'm gonna love you right
I'm gonna take my time,
this could take all night
I'm gonna hug, kiss and squeeze ya' tight
I might growl but I sure don't bite

Girl, I'm gonna whisper in your ear
Say all the things ya love to hear
I may even make you shed a tear
When I say - sugar honey, darling dear

Girl, I'm gonna hold ya in my arms
It's not hot yet but it's gettin warm
I plan to impress ya with my charm
You'll be cackling like ya on the farm

First I'm gonna slo-o-owly undress ya
Second I'm gonna have to test ya
Girl, there ain't no time to rest here
Thirdly, tell the truth, Am I the best? Yeah!

You pass the test, ha, ha, ha

Watch out girl, here I come
Get ready baby, come and get you some
Get all you want, I've got a ton
The wait is over girl, now it's on!

Yeah, that's it, yeah that's right
Girl I'm telling ya
this could take all night
ooo-o-o-o-o-oohs baby!
Ooooo-oh Ms Lady
Ooppppps —so-so-sorry baby (Yeah sorry my ass, you sorry ass)
Just gimme a minute, Im'a make this up to ya
ZZZ-Z-Z-z-z-z-z-zzzzZ-Z-Z-Z-Z-

z-z-z-z-z-z-z-z-z-z-z-z-z-

ZZZZZZZZZZZ-zpzpzp-zzzzzzzzzZZZZ

The morning after…
7:30 a.m, his breath reeking of bullsh-t

Ya 'awful quiet baby
Didn't I rock your world?
I know, you're speechless
That's alright li'l girl

I'll try to get by here sometime
Yeah girl, like I told ya
that was mighty fine.

No! Please don't come by
Please don't call
I promise, I won't be mad at all
Forget the things I said I craved
First thing Sunday morning I'm getting Saved
I'm sure it's time for me to start to live right
I'm not waiting for Sunday, I'm going Wednesday night

Now Lord,
Surely, I don't need to ask for
Forgiveness for that?
I truly suffered, I was punished
I paid the price
I'm sure I made a sacrifice…huh?
OK, first thing, sorry

RUFUS EARL

Ms Cynthia

There're very few women in this world
Who haven't encountered a Rufus Earl
The kind of guy that's always there
Walks around without a single care
Walks really slow; takes his time
Smiles and always says he's fine

Rufus is a woman's handy man
The one that always understands
Never gets fresh or asks for pay
Says he doesn't mind, it was on his way
You can talk to Rufus about your man
He nods and says again, he understands
But girls beware, that's just their plan
All Rufus Earl's have a master plan

I'd met this beautiful man – an Adonis
He was full of lies and a shallow promise
But sisters you should see this man
So hot you'll take your hand and fan
He looks so scrumptious and delicious
Fit, fine, no calories, nutritious

My expensive perfume and best lingerie
No, not a problem – "Adonis please stay"
Like all good things; they come to an end
Adonis met his end before he could begin

To be fair; Adonis really did try
His frustration made me want to cry
I bid Adonis bye and ask my girlfriend why?
Why, why, can't I find the right guy?

So, who shows up but Rufus Earl
I needed someone to rock my world
I'd tried pretty boys; why not a dufus?
If I owed anybody, it certainly was Rufus
Rufus would repair my car or sink
I figured Rufus would probably stink
(was I ever wrong to think) cont…

All the time Rufus was hanging around
Who knew Rufus was hanging down?
Rufus handled me like a precious pearl
He totally blew my mind; I felt like Mrs. Earl

Ru, Rufus, Rufus Earle you know you're wrong!
I can't believe the way you rocked my thong!
I'm a happy woman, happy as I can be
And thankful for the smell of Rufus Earl on me
I rushed out and got Rufus Earl a key

Rufus Earl blew more than wind up my skirt
And I'm leaving right now to get Rufus Earl "A Shirt
or Something"   (Reference **To My Sisters With Love**)

SLEEPING WITH PETE

Ms Cynthia

Started work today, seems really nice
Dresses well, no respect for price
This finger might be wearing ice
Soon you might be throwing rice
OK, *bird seed, whatever*
Body fine, yes, nice behind
Thick and round, just my kind
I hope he's single, I don't want to cheat
But I want to sleep with this man named Pete

These hoochies will be trying too
I need a clear plan of what to do
Sue, could never be his boo
And I can mark off Rena too
I do worry about Ms Heather
anybody's body, any kind of weather
Then I thought - maybe Kay
any ol' how and any ol' way
Then I said I'd better watch Betty

In Vicky's Secrets for that just right teddy
Not much worried about Miss Missy
She's too huggy, feely and kissy
Sheila won't stop cussing and yelling
Barbara just keeps kissing and telling
And of course I can cross off Pam
She likes girls and couldn't give a damn

I gotta stay close on his case,
Find the secret to this man's space
It's so difficult; he works on this job
Like any diva, I called my gay friend Bob

Girl, you won't believe what Bob said
I sat straight up in the bed
What Bob told me was really deep
That's why I called you
This wouldn't keep
I can't go back to sleep
Is this a load, a great big heap?
That bitch Bob is sleeping with Pete
Skank!

Business Matters

Ms Cynthia

How well I remember the struggle known as **"Women's Lib"**. We fought so hard to be accepted into this so-called "man's world". I've got to admit it though, this corporate setup works, actually it rocks!

For you and me, it's a smile-filled "good morning" every work day. We're able to see each other on breaks and exchange glances every chance we get. Often there are opportunities for us to grab lunch together. It's also very necessary that we speak on the phone…most often, very often. Then, the cleaver emails that appear to be business related; so far, people really don't seem to notice a thing.

Actually, that's one of the many things that I admire so much about you, your professional and authoritative manner. It really turns me on. Although, I must admit, I'm no slouch myself.

For instance, your name is on your desk, my name is on mine. You wear power suits, but so do I. You always wear comfortable footwear, and today, so am I. Agreed, I'm the talker, but you're a better listener. OK, so it's true what they say; opposites attract.

I mean, even when we meet for drinks, or dinner, we're relaxed, yet discreet, you know, business. For instance, on business trips we're able to comfortably stay together as long as we are registered in separate rooms. Two expense accounts are always better than one, right?

Yeah, I've got to admit it, the fight to be treated equal in this business world has indeed been worth it. A great career, company benefits, and an opportunity to respect each other, learn from each other, climb this corporate ladder together while holding hands on the way up. Just us two, I love it and I love you.

Now, whatever will we do if our husbands find out?

VIDEO DIVA/SHAKE DANCE QUEEN

MS CYNTHIA

"Shake, shake, shake your body - Oh girl, don't hurt nobody
Yes girl, you're a star - I'm sure you'll go far
Go girl, make that money – This here's 'Big Money Johnny'
Shake, shake, shake it nice – Of course he'll buy you ice!"

Shake your body girl
Oh yeah, you've got it girl
You're so gorgeous girl
They're just jealous girl

"Girl, you sure are fine
You've got an awesome grind
Of course, you've got a mind
And a nice behind"

"Roll your body girl,
Let 'em see you dance
You've got a tender body
You don't need romance"

"This music doesn't stop
Drop, do the booty whop
Now take it to the floor
You got it! Show some more"

"What'ya doin here?
For real? You dancin' here?
Can you get me a beer?
Ashamed? Come here"

"This ain't no happenstance
Can I get a dance?
Come on, this is me
Is this one for free?"

"Hey, this here is Tom
We just saw your mom
They say you suck your thumb
That's sure to make Tom cum…
back"

"Man remember her
Super-fine. Yes sir!
A's on all her test
Damn, did you see her chest?"

"You sure are moving girl
You keep it grooving girl
You sure are sweet
Where you dancing next week?"

"Yes girl, ride that pole
So what the F-ck it's cold
Remember what you're told
Be brazen, rough and bold"

"She's got a little boy
By a dude named Troy
I didn't stand a chance
Now I watch her dance"

"It's a money game"
"I know, ain't it a shame"?
"Now she's a nasty girl"
"Nawh bro, an ashy girl"

*Oh, the lights are bright
You'll shake it all night
A star at legal age
Always loved the stage*

"Shake, shake, shake Ms Thing
Show off that g-string
Count your money girl
You showed your honey girl!"

"Hey Ms Shake It Girl
We're going round the world
You just might make it girl
'Cause you be 'twerkin' girl
"No tellin' how many maps
No tellin' how many laps
No tellin' how many raps
Mo' money, so many saps!!"

"Where the ballers at?
You know their pockets fat
Come to the booty bar!
Friday night, you are a star!

*You're on a video?
All night, no dough?
They 'spose to call you though?
They gon' call you a hoe!*

*Hey, it's the after party
Drinking, sniffing, getting naughty
You want to make it girl?
Get butt-naked girl
"Bend over take it girl
Now yell and fake it girl*

His rockets to the moon
You made him cry a tune"
"Hey, why do you holla?
Hell, you made a dolla'
Us you chose to follow
You didn't even swallow"

"Go on, shake it girl
One day you'll make it girl
We're headed round the world
We just can't take you girl"

Now put your clothes on
Now you can go on
Why're you on the phone?
"I need…"
You need a ride home?"

Said they loved you girl
Said they dug you girl
Tried to drug you girl
Said you were bugging girl

Yeah, you made 'em smile
They laughed and grinned awhile
"Girl, why do you weep?
Played and feeling weak
A lover you can't keep
Why? You let the guys peep"

10 years later...

Your breasts have let you down
Your butts no longer round
The men now laugh or frown
They treat you like a clown
You were a shake it girl
You let them tape you girl
Don't let 'em break you girl
Your life; take it girl
Break out and make it girl

Domestic
&
Social ILLS

What's wrong with That Girl?

Written by Ms Cynthia

You question what's wrong with me?
Open your eyes, what do you see?
A girl living in misery
Struggling, trying to set myself free

"Her parents buy her everything"
"She's such a spoiled little thing"
Since forever, computers, clothes and toys
All she seems to think of are boys"

You say I should respect myself
Every night I tried to protect myself
Thanks dad, you made me reject myself
Now I've started to inject myself
Maybe I'll disconnect myself…

It's getting harder and harder to take
Riding me like a horse he's trying to break
Wrestling, scuffling and scrambling for headroom
Panicking for breath in my own bedroom

Mom pretends she's fast asleep
Why in the hell did she marry this creep?
Tells her he's going to tuck me in
I'm just thirteen – he's tucking it in
My head begins to spin, and spin

He's raped me again, again, and again,
Back again, please no, not again!

Remember, I was telling "Daddy No!"
Trying then to tell you so
I grew older it didn't stop
Who wants this love from her Pop?

Pop, bleed went this little girl's pearl
Told it was precious, my precious bloody pearl
Zoom, zoom goes my gloomy room
Twirl, whirl goes this little girl's world
Thought it would be gentle and kind
This windstorm called life blows my mind
Pop, pop, pop each and every time goes my mind

Never again, he won't have control
Not my mind, body and soul
You'll see wild, crazy and bold
Yes, my sisters, I'm taking a-hold

Yes, I'm quite conspicuous
Yes, I'm even promiscuous
Giving it to whomever, whenever I want
No longer will I let him taunt - just being blunt

Mom knew it was likely to occur
You see, her dad did the same thing to her
Oblivious that this devil would reappear
Not to worry, this generational demon stops here

You, you judged me when I ran away
Never support, you had plenty to say
I was trying to keep him away
I'm back; he's back, wanting to play

So please don't ask what's wrong with me
Free now as a bird you see
Drugging, sexing, being all I can be
No help, so I set myself free

Drugs help to stop the pain
Escape the endless nights of shame
Daddy's power no longer reigns
He's gone, won't ever do it again

Whirl, whirl went my mind,
Remembering all those awful times
He took away my little girl's pearl
He destroyed my little girl's world…Never again!

Pop, pop, pop! Down went my Pop
Lucky for me he wasn't on top
His pain, his blood on my bed
On my rug, on my spread, "man its red"!
"Oopps, sorry, my bad" my mom sobbingly said
"Officer, I thought it was a prowler, is he dead?

WHO'S UNCLE JOHN AND AUNT IVA?

MS CYNTHIA

Who are Uncle John and Aunt Iva? You're kidding right? Why, they live in most cities and towns.

Aunt Iva is a sweet lady that smiles and speaks to everyone. She has four children, two sons and two daughters.

You can see her at the bus stop every morning, rain or shine, going to her house- keeping job. She's as dedicated to her job as she is to her family and church. You can see her with her daily bag of groceries; she shops daily because she doesn't drive and can't afford a taxi.

Aunt Iva is quite shy and often wears a scarf or hat. She even wears long sleeves in the summer months. If you look past her smile, you can see bruises she's hiding from only God knows what. If you look even closer there's bruising and swelling on her wrist, neck, ankles and face. Her wrist is often wrapped in an ace bandage; so is her ankle more often than not. She also wears sun glasses to protect her eyes from the sunlight, even in Winter. Yes, Aunt Iva is some kind'a woman, mother and dedicated wife.

Uncle John? Surely, you've seen him in your town. He's either at his woman's house with their two kids or he's at home in his daughter's room day or night, smelling of alcohol, committing incest. No dating for these girls, they belong to daddy. If you look into their eyes you can see clearly that their souls are hiding. No problem, Aunt Iva knows about it all. She say's "we all make mistakes, and he's still my husband. I'll stand on my marriage vows until I die."

His sons, he says, are queer and anyone can see it, at least one of them. He could always tell "from the day she brought that boy home from the hospital." He wasn't doing anything that wasn't going to happen to him anyway, after all, just like his daughters, that was his son.

His older boy left home long before graduating high school. He couldn't take the mental or physical abuse anymore. The tears from his mom, sisters and his brother were more than he could tolerate. He thought often of ending it all.
He thought about it a lot, but didn't have the nerve - but he was tired and maybe one day…someday.

One day Aunt Iva came home and no one seemed to be there. The girl's door was open. She didn't see or hear them. She looked in her room and didn't see or hear her daughters or her husband. He normally came staggering out of the girl's room tugging at his pants, which she always ignored, but today, there was no sign of any of them. She called out their names and no one answered. Finally she looked into the bathroom and to her shock she saw her husband lying naked in a pool of blood on the floor.

She looked up over the sink and saw a bloodied handprint on the mirror, it wasn't very large, not large enough to be her husbands.

She left the bathroom to call the police for the first time in her life, whatever would they think?

The police arrived, finally, and began to investigate the scene. They asked Aunt Iva questions about her family, their where-a-bouts and personal family business. How dare they? She knew they wouldn't have dared ask that if her husband was alive. She had been raised to keep quiet since she began to have secrets as a child. Anything that went on in her house should not be spoken of in public, nothing. She vowed to keep that promise early on and she would, no matter what, she always had. It was none of their business. They just needed to find out what happened to her husband. That was their only job and purpose in her home.

After dusting, sweeping, magnifying and asking questions, the officers could not figure out what had happened in this house to this man. They asked Aunt Iva where her girls were and she told them she had no idea. That seemed normal to the officers since most parents don't know where their teenage daughters are, but Aunt Iva knew it was strange. She always knew where her girls were – there for their father – always. They asked about her sons and she answered the same, she had no idea. What the officers didn't know was that her son never came home until late because he hated his father's put-downs and brutal behavior.

The officers asked Aunt Iva who cleaned the bathroom, it was quite obvious that someone had recently disinfected and cleaned the area where her husband was found. Aunt Iva confessed that she cleaned the bathroom when she found her husband because he would be very upset if anyone saw their bathroom in such a mess, a bloody mess.

She had picked up, cleaned up and thrown away everything that was out of place so her husband wouldn't be mad or embarrassed if he should wake up. The officers shook their heads in disbelief. "She cleaned up all the evidence. There's nothing here but a dead body. No witnesses, no weapon and no clues, all because she thought she was being a good wife? What a shame" the officer said. "Do you think she did it? She did catch the trash man since he was running late, everything is gone except this naked man."

After the officers left, Aunt Iva sat down and thought. What could have happened here? She realized almost anything could have happened and who was she to judge whoever did it or how it happened. She knew her children would not be able to overlook or forgive their father's abuse as she had so many years. She thought of different possible scenarios, but decided to think about it later and just cook dinner. Since she had already cleaned her bathroom, she would finish cleaning the rest of her house and prepare for bed as she always did, after all, tomorrow was another work day. In the morning she would shower, get dressed, put on her scarf, walk to the bus stop, go to her job and pick up groceries on her way home.

THE END

AND THE BEAT GOES ON

Ms Cynthia

Dad's hung over, goes to work
Boss —a tyrant, treats him like dirt
Fired on the spot, dad's pride is hurt
Boss rips dad's name off his shirt
Somebody is gonna get hurt
wife needs to be on alert
The heat is on and the beat goes home…

Dad gets home, wife's on the phone
begging her folks for another loan
"Why don't you just come home?"
"What the hell?" It's dang-sure on!
He's really pissed and the beat goes on…

He's wet from life's angry sweat
And his doggone dinner ain't ready yet
Another a- - kicking for her? You bet!
And the beat goes on and on and on…

Mom's bruised, awful pain
feeling hurt and so ashamed
Kids running, screaming fits
Mom's swollen from fists and kicks
Fed up, she grabs a stick
Kids screaming from hard licks
Mama please! She can't seem to quit
son won't cry but his lip is bit
And the beat goes on and on…

Sends her kids off to school,
Kid's are mean; jokes are cruel
son is sick and tired of it,
he ain't taking no more sh-t
An innocent child is stomped and kicked
And the beat goes on and on and on…

Son is sent to Juvenile
Where he's going to be awhile
Even though he's just a child
He's going to be sexed buck wild
Meaner boys that have walked that mile
And the beat goes on and on and on

Son is grown, finally out
Still poor, trouble waits; no doubt
As fate would have it, he finds a wife
A daughter, two sons; her previous life
He molest her daughter and younger son
The older son has his dad's gun
A gift before leaving on the run

Wife is beaten protecting her son
Son calls the cops and gets his gun
shoots the gun, an awful sound
Stunned step-dad falls to the ground
Son is handcuffed and beaten down
This beat just goes around and round
And the beat goes on and on and on…

A beat that never lets 'em down
Future generations can sense that sound
Can't you hear it? *pound, pound, pound*
Smell the anger; it's about to go down
Sometimes it pop, pop, pop
Sounds that never seem to stop
Even when it pow, pow, pow
The kids want us to stop it now!!!
"Ain't none of my business anyhow"
So the beat goes on and on
and on…
and on…
and on…

THE COLOR WAS RED

MS CYNTHIA

Visions of sugar plums
danced in her head –
frosty purplish red
lilies, daises, sunflowers, tulips
peonies and roses – red

she dreamed of pretty dresses
frilly lace, eyelet, gold thread
white socks, ribbons, beads
a birthstone ring – garnet red

abruptly awaken, eyes slightly red
glanced through the window
clouds, sky, rain - bluish red

push, shove, weight dead
pain, screams, nothing said
sweat, stench, crumbled bed
what? who? why?
shameless aggression fed
flowered sheets stained red

innocence stolen, silent tears shed
confused, dazed, spinning head
color from broken hymen - red

bleeding heart, shattered dreams now red
lying on a table, legs spread
another innocent life shed
two months of hindered blood
returned red

A BAD CASE OF THE A'LEASE-HE

Ms Cynthia

Ladies,

There's a severe case of a common disease going around.
This notice is to inform you of the symptoms so that you'll
be aware. Just know, it's nothing new - it's been around for years.

It's found in every ethnic, age, gender and economic group.
For some strange reason, it seems to affect women more often
than men. But men, please know you are not immune to it.

I ask you at this time to check yourself and your friends to see if
anyone you know is suffering from any of the symptoms listed below.
CAUTION: You may suffer from one or more at a time.

MOST COMMON LIST

A'lease he goes to work and pays the bills even though he hits me
A'lease he doesn't kick me and hit me in the face where people can see
A'lease he takes the time to say he's sorry afterward and helps clean me up
A'lease he cries and tries to do better each time it happens
A'lease he tells me he loves me and that nobody else ever will
A'lease he says that he beats me because he loves me so much; he's just jealous
A'lease he comes home sometimes; that's better than not at all
A'lease he goes looking for work when he's gone in my car all day
A'lease he leaves me enough of my money to buy gas so I can go to work
A'lease he tells me he's got other women so nobody else will have to
A'lease he didn't black my eye; I can get new teeth

A'lease he makes sure that I see him a'lease on the weekends
A'lease he tells me that his wife just doesn't understand him like I do
A'lease he let's me know when I need to go to the health department for shots
A'lease he…didn't kill me… a'lease not this time
A'lease he says he's going to get help and I believe him this time

At least he this and at least he's that. This disease spreads rapidly if not treated.
Get help now for the A'lease-he's or A'lease don't tell us.
We've heard it all before. We still love you; just waiting for you to love yourself.

MRS SOMEBODY III

MS CYNTHIA

I AM MRS. SOMEBODY III
GENERATIONS OF CLASS, I'M SURE YOU'VE HEARD
TO THINK YOU HAVEN'T WOULD SIMPLY BE ABSURD
AFTER ALL, I'M THE WIFE OF MR. SOMEBODY III

I'M SPEAKING ON BEHALF OF THE ONES IN NEED
THIS INFORMATION WILL BRING YOU UP TO SPEED
THERE IS NO FORMALITY, THERE IS NO CREED
I ASK, IF YOU WILL, PLANT A SMALL SEED

I'M RICH AND BLUE-BLOODED AND EDUCATED
I HAVE A FABULOUS HOME AND WELL SITUATED
BUT ENOUGH ABOUT ME, THESE ARE SO POOR
WE'LL EVEN COLLECT AT YOUR FRONT DOOR

THEY REALLY NEED HELP, GIVE IF YOU CAN
ALL WE'RE ASKING IS A HELPING HAND
FOR MAYOR LAST YEAR, MY HUSBAND RAN
WE ALSO HAVE A GREAT FINANCIAL PLAN

OUR CHILDREN ATTEND IVY LEAGUE SCHOOLS
THEY GOLF AND SWIM IN IVY LEAGUE POOLS
THESE POOR PEOPLE DON"T HAVE A THING
WELL, AT LEAST THEY CAN DANCE AND SING

SO SING HALLELUIAH AND CLAP YOUR HANDS

THE HIGH SCHOOL IS SENDING A MARCHING BAND
I MUST GET HOME AS FAST AS I CAN
I'M MEETING WITH THE ORKIN MAN
PESKY TERMITES, YOU DO UNDERSTAND?

WE NEED TO GET THESE PEOPLE OFF DRUGS
WE NEED TO RELIEVE THEIR HOODS FROM THUGS
MARIJUANA, CRACK, ALL KINDS OF STUFF
MALT LIQUOR, CIGARETTES, AND ANGEL DUST

OF COURSE, I DRINK WINE AND A LITTLE BRANDY
ABSOLUTE, WHITE LABEL SCOTCH WHEN IT'S HANDY
VALIUM AND ZOLOFT FOR MY NERVE CONDITION
BUT UNDERSTAND - MY DRUGS ARE PRESCRIPTION
I'VE OVER-INDULGED, SOMEWHAT, WHEN WE'RE OUT
BUT PEOPLE UNDERSTAND, I'M A LADY WITH CLOUT
AT TIMES MY HUSBAND DOESN'T COME HOME
WHAT AM I TO DO WHEN I'M HOME ALONE?

OK, I MIX CRYING WITH LIQUOR AND PILLS
SO WHAT, I CALL MY LAWYER AND CHANGE MY WILL
AND YES, I GO TO REHAB WHEN THERE'S NO REFILLS
OH MY GOODNESS, I'M SO SAD AND BLUE
YA' KNOW, THAT'S WHAT BLUE-BLOOD WILL DO
BUT SAVE THESE PEOPLE, WON'T YOU COME
THROUGH?

OH DEAR GOD, WHAT'S WRONG WITH ME?
THESE PEOPLE NEED ME, CAN'T YOU SEE
THIS SIMPLY CAN NOT BE HAPPENING TO ME

LOOK – THEY CAN SEE STRAIGHT THROUGH ME?

STRAIGHT TALK
Featuring Sis Lula Mae Davis

    Honey, you just foolin' yourself
    You ain't better than nobody else
    Only one way to be a Who's who
  Recognize all God's children are somebody too
    You standing there talking just like a fool
   Who cares where your kids attended school?
    Tell God if you lifted somebody up?
  Who cares how much you get from your pre-nup
    Sit down, listen here and hush up

  It's good to help people, but help yourself
  Honey, you're a victim even with wealth
  We all need help from North to South
Get off that high horse and stop running your mouth
Love somebody, hug somebody, and help somebody too
  Every time you do, it happens back to you
  A little more rehab might be good for you too
NOW THAT'S THE WORD MRS III

MOMMY HE HURTS ME – The letter

MS CYNTHIA

DEAR MOMMY,

He hurts me when you're gone. He told me not to tell you, please don't tell I told mommy, please.

Mommy he said he would hurt you and I believe him. He said it wouldn't hurt but it does hurt mommy and I don't like it. He does nasty things to me and tells me not to ever tell anyone. He tells you that I've been bad and he sent me to my room. Mommy I hate my room now. Can I have another room one day? Can we move away? He said if I told you would send me away. Please don't send me away mommy. I love you mommy but, he hurts me when you're gone.

He said I shouldn't be a big cry baby.
He said I cry like a little girl.
He said I should grow up and understand that he provides for us.
He said we would be poor and homeless without him. He said I should do this with him because he makes you happy. I want you to be happy. I don't like to see you cry and be sad when you don't have nobody to love you but I love you. Can't we just move away? I can get a job. I'm almost ten years old now.

Mommy I don't like myself anymore and I want to run away but I don't want to leave you. I want to tell my real daddy but he said my real daddy doesn't love me because he left us. Is that true mommy? I want to be grown up and not cry but Mommy he hurts me and makes me do nasty stuff when you're gone. I don't want to do it anymore. I'm sorry mommy. Please don't be mad at me.

Your son

Cause of Death – A Broken Heart
Her song

Ms Cynthia

She experienced a hard life from a very early age. For whatever reason, she'd been separated from her family, she never said why. She also never said if her recollection of family included her mom and dad; she did, however, mention siblings. She and one sister found themselves in foster care together. She spoke vaguely about the devastation of being in the foster care system. She, like a lot of kids, was moved often from place to place. The things she didn't describe caused her face to drop with anguish when recalling what she had decided long ago not to ever speak of. It was very clear and quite obvious that she had also challenged herself not to revisit those times and places. But as we all know, memories can be hardheaded. Sometimes they just creep in when you're at your most vulnerable and comfortable.

Once she spoke of being hanged from the ceiling in a barn by one of her foster parents. She must have been hanging by her arms, because she said it involved a naked beating. The things that took place in that barn, on more than one occasion, were occurrences of severe brutality that a young girl, or anyone for that matter, should never imagine or endure. These memories caused her to withdraw from her conversations and quickly move, somewhat dazed, to a less painful topic. She would shy away from speaking about those times, because, no doubt, those times were filled with mind shattering secrets. As I mentioned, it was mostly what she didn't say or the sentences cut short, that spoke the most, that ripped off her mask of contentment to reveal shame and embarrassment.

Then she met you; her Sir Lancelot, her knight in shining armor, her savior. The one who, before God, vowed to love, honor and cherish her as your beloved wife for life. The man who would take away all the hurt and fill her with the love she'd been so desperately seeking. You would be the one to father her children, not just use her sexually like the foster fathers and sons did. You would be the one to finally offer the type of life she knew she was destined to live – finally. She willingly surrendered it all to you.

Initially, you treated her extremely well, most do. You married her, which gave her your name. Thank God, she finally had a name, she was about to be somebody! She was somebody's wife – not just an object of sexual pleasure. Soon she was the mother of your little somebody's. She finally had a family; her very own family. She could relax and be the parental example that was never there for her. The babies she had previously given away, before meeting you, were both in good homes; not in that callous foster care system. They were adopted into loving homes and now she could be happy for the first time in her life; all dependant upon you. To quote from the movie **Malcolm X -** *"That's just too much power for one man to have."* Obviously, that was the case with you.

When I saw her, I noticed old scaring on her face. I thought perhaps it could be from earlier years; some were. She spoke of you in a loving tone. It was clear she needed to envision what her fairy tale images of family had shown. After enduring so much anguish and tragedy in her youth, maybe you were the lesser of two evils. It was evident that she had convinced herself so.

I observed you closely because I could feel that what she was saying and what her bruising was conveying were total opposites. Indeed, time would tell.

I visited her more and more often because she was such a pleasant person to be around. She smiled a lot, showing those deep dimples; my oldest son has dimples just like hers. She laughed from a place where you didn't exist. She spoke of current events and such, rarely speaking of the grief in her home. She never mentioned the beatings or constant mistreatment from you. She only mentioned you had lots of women. She only spoke of them because they would call on the phone while I was visiting with her. She was so cordial to them. It was clear why they felt so comfortable calling. She would even ask if they'd like to leave a message. It was as if she took some sense of pride in being the one answering the phone, as your wife, and that your women friends had to come through her.

Thinking back, I wouldn't have known how dastardly you were, had your own children not told me how you mistreated their mother. I noticed that they had very little respect for her; that somewhat explained why. I asked her once about the healed cut above her lip and she dropped her head and said it was the result of a previous fight. She didn't realize that it wasn't a fight but rather domestic abuse. A fight involves parties hitting, not one party hitting and the other receiving the licks. The kids even told me how you would throw them around once they were old enough to help get you off her.

I recall you bragging about the way you worked so hard to support your family and how she didn't have to work and should be proud to have a man like you. You certainly had convinced her of that; but by not being employed, she was totally dependant upon you. Whatever you threw out, she caught, knowing she had no other family and no where else to turn with five children. People always say "get out" but none of their doors are open.

I realized in talking with her that a woman who feels trapped in a situation, without a reasonable way out, can train her mind and body to adapt. She can smile through the pain of verbal and even physical abuse. She'd also realized that the more she cried, pleaded and begged, the more empowered you became. Her learned survival tricks were initially fascinating, even amazing to me. She, with mental strength, had taught her body to cave long before the hits, kicks and stomps. She trained her face to bleed and her eye to swell before you ever took a swing.

She learned to tune you out long before the name calling even began. Better yet, she tried teaching her heart to never break, though it would ached, allowing her to stay for her children knowing not to expect anything better from you. In your hateful attempts to belittle her before her children and friends; constant ridicule, put downs and name calling, I noticed something enlightening; she wasn't allowing you to break her. Her unbroken spirit led her to bear it all and continue smiling. But what we didn't see was she was actually dying inside.

Yes, you continued to kill her everyday – slowly. Your words were cruel and selfish. You made every attempt to make sure she felt worthless. Her physical beauty began to show signs of wear; the old bruises and traces of burning tears over many nights and days of sadness were finally noticeable. Her bright smile had begun to turn downward. As stated earlier – time would tell – the sands in the hour glass were revealing a hurtful truth.

Your reign of terror was finally taking its toll on her soul. She was tired and reluctantly giving in. She was finally showing signs of defeat; you refused to let up, even a little. Your shouting shattered her womanly warmth. Your mere presence was violence begging for a flicker of controversy, waiting to explode like a time bomb – tick, tick, "come on somebody, piss me off", tick. Your volcano was always ready to erupt hot burning lava all over your home to let them all know who was boss under your roof. "I will kill all of you m&^%$ f##@^* in this house. Don't f^*#@ play with me!" Your children seemed to learn from you that shouting and violence would earn them respect; it's no wonder they found themselves in futile situations beyond their control.

I've heard men like you bragg - "After all, my dad did it and my mama took it. Ain't no woman better than my mama and every son wants to be just like his dad". "Ah hell, she's still living ain't she? If I wanted her dead, she would be!" "She's alright. She's still breathin, if only barely. Ha, ha, I told you, I don't play!" "A good ass whipping ain't never hurt nobody, it's actually good for women. Got to keep them bitches in line or they'll whip your ass if you ain't careful" "She's going to do what the hell I tell her, when I tell her, or I'm going to beat her ass 'til she does. And I don't give a damn about going to jail. Call the damn cops. "I'm the man of my house, understand? I'll kill her ass and I promise you I won't serve one damn day – watch me. I know people; ask her, she'll tell you. She knows I'll do it!"

She finally left you; well actually, you left her. She made up her mind to divorce you. Your plans didn't go as you'd hoped; nobody else was going to put up with you, so you returned. Not only did she take you back, her fairy tale dreams of love returned and she remarried you. She was so sure that you would finally appreciate her after the other women had let you down. But again, disillusioned, she was faced with the reality that nothing about you had changed. Again, she would wear the pain from your bitterness.

At last, she moved away - you bid her farewell. After years of being battered and finally broken she made an attempt to salvage whatever pride she had left. With little sense of direction or functioning life skills, she sought no longer for true happiness but for a place of peace, tranquility and spirituality. She left behind the life that had failed her wandering aimlessly into a world that was cold, bitter and uncaring. She surely must have found some sense of comfort out there because it was such a reminder of her life with you. Disconnected, confused and alone she finally allowed her heart to break for the very last time. She died of heart failure. She left only one request for her children to complete; to have her body cremated. You even objected to that. It was all about control with you. She never asked for much, only to be loved. I guess, again, you can brag – In your own way – you loved her to death.

Once I was asked by a teenage girl if someone could die from a broken heart. I looked into her sad eyes and said to her "Well baby, I not absolutely sure, but I think so."

To my sisters who want and need love so desperately in your lives; a sense of family, or "I can't give in because they tried to tell me so", "I'm sure I can make this work if I can just prove to him that I'll stand by him", or whichever a'lease-he you suffer from, this is what men like him often provide.

Their low self esteem and insecurity appears to drive them into a semblance of madness. They tend to take it out on the only one that has ever made a sincere attempt to love them – that would be you. Their task seems to be - to prove they really aren't worth your love. They continue to drive that point home, in your home, with you and your children time and time again.

Sisters, this is a sickness. If you continually find yourself in this type of situation, search yourself to see why you have a tolerance for, or seem to attract this type of man. Yes, it's on you; your choices. This sickness definitely doesn't apply to all men, not even most men – so why is it only your men?

Ask yourself the hard questions: Why would I stay in something that demeans my very existence? What type of example am I exhibiting before my children – daughters and sons? Is this the attitude and behavior I want my girls to emulate and have tolerance for? Am I the type of woman I want my sons to be attracted to and seek out? Only you know.

Sisters, know that God loves you. He created us to nurture and love, show love and be loved. Also know you deserve a mate that's committed to bringing forth real love into your life. How will you recognize real love? Girl -**Real Love doesn't hurt!**

HIV/AIDS

Ms Cynthia

Could have happened to anyone of us
Standing with you, in this please trust
Hug you and love you by day and night
We may still cuss, fuss and fight
That's still alright, friendship still tight

'Cause we won't treat you differently
Well, maybe a little more lovingly
AID/HIV - more than alphabets
Recognizing it's a dreadful disease people get

If you find yourself feeling confused
Find yourself feeling misused
Keep fighting, you can't afford to lose
We've got to row this boat; it's not a luxury cruise

Some say its careless sexual behavior
Others, that it's your sexual flavor
Some were protected; got it anyway
Husband, boyfriends, straight and gay

Some contracted through blood transfusion
Talk TV causing more confusion
Sure, some contracted from prostitution
So know it's real, not an illusion

Surely some were drug addicted
Found themselves also afflicted
Aggressive disease that's transmitted
We've got to be more aggressively committed

Not one of us lives a life that's pure
Remember prayer and love, that's for sure
Support the afflicted that have to endure
Be more determined to help find a cure

H EED PRECAUTIONS
  I NFORM YOURSELF OF RISK
    V OICE YOUR SUPPORT FOR VICTIMS
      A TTEND AWARENESS GROUPS
        I SOLATE IGNORANT GOSSIP
          D ISCOVER NEW WAYS TO BE OF HELP
            S UPPORT AN INFECTED FRIEND

Keep Your Hands to Yourself

To My Sisters,

Would you, could you, please stop hitting, smacking and fighting men simply because they won't hit you back? It's not cute, OK.

Women have gone through hell and back just to get protection from law enforcement for physical and domestic abuse. The last thing we need is a woman abusing a man, showing off, because he won't hit her back. It works both ways.

Some mothers actually taught their sons not to ever hit a woman. Having said that, don't take that to mean you have clearance to hit, curse and embarrass him and yourself in public, or in private for that matter (your business right?)

Typically, I'm not so blunt or to the point about a particular matter, but this one really sets a bad tone for woman-kind. We're better than that.

If you are fortunate enough to have a man in your life that will walk away from disagreements – please allow him to do so, and realized how blessed you are. It's not that he fears you, understand that he respects you, himself and the female or male who taught him to respect women as he would like to see his mother or sister respected.

Thanks for listening; I really needed to get that out.

Always in Love,
Ms Cynthia

CRACK JONES, BAD TO THE BONE
Accompanied by a smokin bass

Ms Cynthia

DISCLAIMER

DO NOT READ

IF YOU ARE NOT PREPARED TO FACE
THE REALITY OR ENTER THIS WORLD OF
CRACK COCAINE

THE HARSH WORDS ARE
NECESSARY TO UNMASK
CRACK IN ITS TRUEST FORM

WHAT CRACK DOES TO A MAN IS VICIOUS
BUT IT'S EFFECTS ON A WOMAN ARE MAGNIFIED
THE WORDS ARE AS GRAPHIC AS
NECESSARY TO REVEAL THIS
DEAMON FROM HELL KNOWN AS

CRACK

"Come on in, trust me.
Believe me, I don't discriminate — all are welcome
regardless of race, gender or economic status —
You have my word — CRACK JONES"

CRACK JONES, BAD TO THE BONE
ACCOMPANIED BY A SMOKIN (BASE)

MS CYNTHIA

THE NAME IS CRACK JONES
YEAH, I'M BAD TO THE BONE
NO, YOU DON'T WANT NONE OF ME
I'M AS BAD AS CAN BE

I'M A BAD, BAD BOY
DON'T MISTAKE ME FOR A TOY
BABY, I'M COOL AS A FAN
YOU'LL BE LEAVING THAT GOOD MAN

I'M PROVEN TIME AND TIME AGAIN
DON'T GIVE A DAMN WHERE YOU BEEN
MUCH LESS WHO YOU ARE
WITH ME YOU'LL BE ASTAR
NO BRAGGIN; JUST FACT
NO DIPLOMACY, NO TACT
I TOLD YOU, I'M CRACK JONES
TRY ME, ENTER MY ZONE, zone, zone....

YOU AIN'T SMOKED NOTHIN LIKE ME
YOUR DOOR IS LOCKED? I'VE GOT THE KEY
YOU'LL BE SELLIN YOUR TV
STEALIN FROM YOUR FAMILY

GIRL, I'LL TAKE ALL YOU GOT
YOU THINK YOU'VE GOT A LOT?
I'LL LIE AND TELL YOU YOU'RE HOTT
YOU'LL HAPPILY BRING ME ALL YOU GOT

I'LL HAVE YOU CRAWLING ON YOUR KNEES
DIGGIN, SNIFFIN, CRYING "PLEASE!"
GIRL, MY NAME IS CRACK JONES
YOU'LL GIVE ME EVERYTHING YOU OWN!

OK, GIVE ME A TRY
IT'S OBVIOUS YOU WANT TO DIE
FIRST I'LL DRAG YOUR ASS DOWN
ALL OVER THIS DAMN TOWN
I TOLD YOU **I'M CRACK JONES**
YOUR PIMP; BAD TO THE BONE

WATCH, I'LL TURN YOUR EYES RED
YOU'LL LOOK LIKE THE WALKIN DEAD
ROT YOUR TEETH, THEN HAVE YOU SMILE
FOLKS WILL SHREAK; "YOUR BREATH IS FOUL"

TOO CRACKED OUT TO TAKE A SHOWER
KNOWING WELL YOUR ASS IS SOUR
LIPS LOOKIN LIKE BABY POWDER
LIKE YOU BEEN KISSIN FLOUR
CHASIN MY HIGH BY THE HOUR, *HOUR, HOUR*

BITCH, I'M YOUR WORST ENEMY
YOU'LL DO ANYTHING FOR ME

SELL YOUR KIDS SEXUALLY
COME TO ME – I'LL SET YOU FREE

COME, TRY ME IF YOU WILL
I'VE BEEN KNOWN TO MAKE 'EM KILL
MAKE YOU WISH YOU WERE DEAD
A PLAYED –OUT, STANK- ASS, CRACK- HEAD

YOU'LL SCRATCH FOR NICKLES AND DIMES
HEAR THE NEWS; THOSE CRIMES ARE MINE
YOU'LL SCRATCH WHEN THERE'S NO ITCH
JUST LIKE YOUR DADDY – HE WAS MY BITCH, HA-*ha*

YOU WERE MUCH TO GOOD FOR THIS
YOU CAN'T EVEN GET A KISS
SIMPLY THREW AWAY YOUR LIFE
YOUR MAN'S GOT ANOTHER WIFE

I'LL TELL YOU **"SHAKE IT FAST"**
I'LL MAKE YOU SELL THAT PRETTY ASS
I'LL HAVE YOUR ASS DOING TRICKS
BEHIND AN ALLEY SUCKIN DICKS

YEAH, CRACK JONES IS THE NAME
STEALIN SOULS, THAT'S MY GAME
I'LL HAVE YOU GOIN INSANE
YOUR FOLKS WONDERING WHO TO BLAME

TOO CUTE TO GO TO SCHOOL
YOU GAVE UP LIKE A FOOL

SUCKED ON ME **CRACK JONES!**
LOOKIN LIKE A BAG OF BONES

WALKED AWAY AND LEFT YOUR KIDS
SOLD THEIR SEX; THE HIGHEST BID
DSS WON'T GIVE 'EM BACK
AND YOU'RE STILL SMOKIN CRACK?

WEREN'T YOU ONCE A BEAUTY QUEEN?
THOUGHT THAT WAS YOU I SEEN
GIRL, THEY HAD BIG PLANS FOR YOU
THAT'S OK, I DO TOO

YOU'RE GOIN BACK TO JAIL AGAIN
BACK INTO THAT CELL AGAIN
SHAKIN LIKE A SKELETON
PARENTS MAKIN BAIL AGAIN
**YOU'RE OUT – BACK IN HELL AGAIN AND AGAIN
I TOLD YOU, YOU CAN'T WIN!**

YOU LOVE ME LIKE THAT!!!!

I TAKE 'EM ALL SHAPES AND SIZES
BIG GIRLS I MINIMIZES
NOT MY FAULT, CAN'T YOU SEE
I WAS CHILLIN, YOU CAME TO ME!

COME HERE MY SENORITA
GIRL, PUT DOWN THAT MARGARITA
I LOVE YOU MAMA-SITA
YOU LITTLE HOT JALAPENO

HEY LITTLE GEISHA GIRL
YOU CAME CLEAN AROUND THE WORLD
TO RUN INTO THE LIKES OF ME
CRUSHIN TRADITION AND FAMILY

BUT HEY, I DO FEEL BAD THOUGH
YOU ALL LOOKED GOOD BEFORE YO'
THOUGHT YOU COULD HANDLE ME?
LOOK AROUND COULDN'T YOU SEE?

OH, YOU CALLIN REHAB?
HOW YOU GETTING THERE - A CAB?
LEAVING ME, DON'T YOU DARE
YOU'LL BE TRICKIN TO PAY YOUR FARE

BITCH, GET OFF THAT TELEPHONE
THEY KNOW I'M BAD TO THE BONE
**YOU'LL BE DISCOLORED AND RUSTY,
A NASTY BITCH AND DUSTY
THE NAME IS CRACK JONES
I'LL SUCK THE MARROW FROM YOUR BONES!**

YOU'VE PRETTY MUCH SEALED YOUR DOOM
SOON HEADED TO YOUR TOMB
LOOK AT YA' – IN FULL BLOOM
DAMN NEAR BARKIN AT THE MOON

I AIN'T GONNA NE-E-VER LEAVE YOU ALONE
SO HANG UP THAT DAMN PHONE
YOU'RE IN THE TWILIGHT ZONE, ZONE, ZONE
I'LL NEVER SET YOU FREE
REMEMBER - YOU CAME TO ME
THAT'S WHERE YOUR ASS IS GONNA BE!
Ha ha ha aaaaaaaaa

At her lowest she remembers her grandmother telling her that GOD will always deliver his children and she cries out…

"DEAR GOD HELP ME PLE-E-E-E-E-E-E-ASE! I NEED YOU LORD, I CAN'T DO IT BY MYSELF. I SURRENDER ALL TO YOU. COME INTO MY LIFE NOW LORD. PLEASE FORGIVE ME OF MY SINS, I'M SORRY. TAKE THIS DEAMON AWAY LORD, I KNOW YOU CAN; I TRUST YOU WILL – RIGHT NOW LORD, IN JESUS NAME AMEN"

GO ON GIRL AND PRAY,
DON'T NOTHIN GET IN MY WAY
HEAR ME? – WHAT'D I SAY?

NO SATAN BELIEVE WHAT I SAY

NOW, THIS IS HOW IT'S GOING TO BE
SATAN, SURELY TO GOD, YOU REMEMBER ME

LISTEN HERE CRACK JONES
I COULD BREAK YOUR BONES
COULD STEP ON YOUR HEAD
YOU'D WISH YOU WERE DEAD

I CAME FOR HER TODAY
ALL SHE HAD TO DO WAS PRAY
I LET HER CHOOSE THE RIGHT WAY
NOTHING LEFT FOR YOU TO SAY

KNOW - THIS IS NOT A FIGHT
I AM THE WAY, THE TRUTH AND LIGHT
WITH A NAME LIKE CRACK JONES
ALL YOU KNOW AND DO IS WRONG

CHILD, JUST CALL OUT MY NAME
THOSE WHO DID KNOW I CAME
STOP YOUR PAIN AND ANGUISH NOW
COME TO ME, I'LL SHOW YOU HOW

DON'T CHASE HIS EVIL HIGH
MY HIGH IS HIGHER THAN HIS HIGH
MY HIGH IS HIGH BEYOND THE SKIES
COME, I'LL DRY YOUR WEEPING EYES

YOUR DAD LEFT YOU ALL ALONE
I'M YOUR FATHER, COME BACK HOME
I DIED FOR YOU AND WAS RISEN
ALL YOUR SINS ARE FORGIVEN

WELL, IT'S OVER CRACK JONES
GO ON, LEAVE MY CHILD ALONE
NOT HER DADDY, I'M HER FATHER
SHE CALLED ME - DON'T EVEN BOTHER

SHE DIDN'T NEED THE TELEPHONE
THIS WOMAN'S SOUL - YOU NEVER OWNED
THIS IS THE END CRACK JONES
BACK TO THAT HELL YOU CALL HOME

COME NOW MY LITTLE GIRL
ENJOY A CALM AND PEACEFUL WORLD
FINALLY YOU CALLED ON ME
RELEASING THAT DEAMON – YOU'RE FREE
HOW CAN YOU REPAY ME?
CONFESS YOUR TESTIMONY; CONTINUE
BELIEVING IN ME

HEY, I AIN'T TRYIN TO HAVE THE LAST WORD
'CAUSE I KNOW **YOU ARE THE WORD**
BUT I TRIED TO TELL HER SO
BUT SHE WOULDN'T LISTEN THOUGH
AND KEEP THIS A SECRET BUT… FOR THE
FIRST TIME - I'M TELLIN THE TRUTH…
ASK HER, SHE'LL TELL YOU…
TELL HIM GIRL, I WAS MINDED MY BUSINESS
AND HERE YOU CAME, money in hand…

BLESSINGS AFFIRMATIONS ENCOURAGEMENT

BLINDED BY THE LIGHT
Which Restored My Sight

Written by Ms Cynthia

Vision clear, thought I'd share
a long road leading nowhere
here, there, everywhere
A lot, little, no time to spare

Up, down, on the ground
nights my head would pound and pound
aching from loud, screaming sounds

Oh yes, having fun
Not someone - anyone
Up all night 'til the sun
Living as if it'd just begun

Laughing, crying, wanting to run
Drugs, alcohol, knives, guns
Tired, burned out, both sides- done
Many friends; seemed like none

And Then... Lo and Behold

Blinded by the Light
couldn't see left or right
couldn't tell day from night
everything was already alright

Wa-a-ay down; lifted up,
dry, thirsty; filled my cup
ashen; anointed my head with oil
now true purpose; work and toil
Fruits of labor from sacred soil

Blind all that time
Darkness; my uncontrived crime
Slothful, wasting valuable time
Ignorant to what was His could be mine

No more rowdiness, acting uncouth
So appreciative I survived my youth
Solid the commitment between Naomi and Ruth
Because of this Light I saw the Truth

Blinded by the Light
I received my sight
The **Son** showed day from night
The dark days took flight

*"I have come into the world as a Light
so that no one who believes in Me should
stay in darkness"* John 12:46

THANK GOD FOR COVERAGE

MS CYNTHIA

so tiny, so pretty
can't get cold
here you are
a blankie trimmed in gold
BABY GIRL COVERAGE

Off to school little one
We're so proud of you
Filling out insurance forms
Praying nothing happens to you
ELEMENTATY SCHOOL COVERAGE

What happened?
All were involved?
On my way right now
We'll get this mess solved!
PARENTS HIGH SCHOOL COVERAGE

Great, your S.A.T.!
financial strain on dad and me
Can't wait to see what you'll be
Education is not free
FUTURE CAREER COVERAGE

Oh, a ring? Really nice
Impressive, fine piece of ice
That wedding dress; what's the price?
A small ceremony would be nice
Surely that would suffice? No chance huh?
BRIDES PARENTS COVERAGE

Many times Lord
Not sure what to do
in your hands
Totally depending on you
Each and every time
You always came through
We continue to thank You and
our daughter does too
FOR YEARS OF DIVINE COVERAGE

LORD, WHERE'S MY CHILD

MS CYNTHIA

Dear Lord,
Please, where's my child?
My husband and I have waited a while

Lord, we've got so much love to give
But none of our babies seem to live

We've been patiently praying, really trying
Can't wait to hear our little baby crying

Lord, speak to me. What must I do?
The only real answer has to come from You

Well, I know of a baby that needs love too
I figure this child would be perfect for you two
I may have others waiting just for you

No need to sit and wait for me
Open your hearts; you'll be able to see
Don't continue to cry and lick your wounds
Your child doesn't have to come from your womb

There're lots of babies out there, every race and kind
Please keep in mind, all children are mine
When you come to the alter, crying down the aisle
There's a baby waiting to be your child

Your child is waiting; Seek, ye shall find
The child that's yours is also Mine
As parents be gentle, stern but kind
Remember - Love is the key and tie that binds

PRAY IT All AWAY

Ms Cynthia

Don't let anyone steal your day
That's one debt they can't repay
You stand firm; it's not OK
Pray, pray trouble away

Wake up, smile at the morning sun
Put on your sneakers, walk if not run
Be thankful from whence you've come
And where the Lord has brought you from
Kick up your heels and have some fun
Not greedy for plenty, but thankful for some
"Some is better than none"
Pray - Lord I thank you for this day

If folks make you angry, bringing you down
Scandalizing your name all over town
Just remember you're Heaven bound
Standing in line for a sacred crown
Ask the Lord to forgive those clowns
Pray all that mess away

Trouble in your way? Walk away
Hold your tears; you're not forced to stay
Like Burger King, let 'em have it their way
Just pray that ignorance away

I don't discount sometimes it's hard,
They let you down, but you've got the Lord
He'll walk with you until you start to run
And thank HIM you don't have a gun

I know what you'd like to say
They'll say "I knew she wasn't Saved anyway"
Just trust God, let HIM have His way
They'll ask for your forgiveness one day
Just say "I did, I prayed it away"

Smile and breathe and silently pray, then blow it all away

Inhale… hold it… let go slowly
Whw-w-w-w-w-w-w-w-w-w-w-w-

Spiritual Healings

Some books were given for our information.
The Bible was given for our transformation.
-Anonymous

Wisdom and knowledge is granted unto thee; and I will give the riches, and wealth, and honour, such as none of the kings have had that have been before thee, neither shall there any after thee have the like. 2 Chronicles 1:12

I will bless the Lord who guides me; even at night my heart instructs me. Psalms 16:7 NLT

The Lord recompense thy work, and full reward be given thee of the Lord God of Israel, under whose wings thou are come to trust. Ruth 2:12

Be careful for nothing; but in every thing in prayer and supplication with thanksgiving let your request be made known unto God. Philippians 4:6

By humility and the fear of the Lord are riches, and honour, and life. Proverbs 22:4

And also that every man should eat and drink, and enjoy the good of all his labour, it is the gift of God. Ecclesiastes 3:13

Let another man praise thee, and not thine own mouth; a stranger, and not thine own lips. Proverbs 27:2

Be not forgetful to entertain strangers: for thereby some have entertained angels unawares. Hebrews 13:2

Better to be of an humble spirit with the lowly, than to divide the spoil with the proud. Proverb 16:19

By humility and the fear of the Lord are riches, and honour, and life. Proverbs 22:4

For I was an hungered, and ye gave me meat: I was thirsty, and ye gave me drink: I was a stranger, and ye took me in:
Naked, and ye clothed me: I was sick, and ye visited me: I was in prison, and ye came unto me.
And the King shall answer and say unto them, Verily I say unto you, Inasmuch as ye have done it unto one of the least of these my brethren, ye have done it unto me. Matthew 25:35-36, 40

For thou art my rock and my fortress; therefore for thy name's sake lead me, and guide me. Psalms 31:3
Thank You God in the Holy Trinity, amen

TO MY SPOKEN WORD SISTERS & BROTHERS

My Book in My Hand

Ms Cynthia

When speaking to audiences
I don't recite
Often comments
about the way I write
oddly unique,
has a slight bite
As I read from my book in my hand

When discussing my books
if you feel the need
Be sure to mention
how well I read
My style, a few can't understand
But they will when they see
my book in my hand

I don't go blank
I have my book in my hand
Not there to recite
I'll have my book in my hand
Not that I'm lazy or contrite
trying to serve this literary plight
Trust me
my readings are out-a-sight
As I read from my book in my hand

Why stand before you
like a wide-eyed fool?
I showcase my book
as a marketing tool?
You rip that mic on demand!
when you end your piece,
I'll snap and stand
But believe, when it's my turn to stand
I'll have my book in my hand

You can judge my book by its cover
It's fresh, real like no other
At times controlling like your mother
but love-filled
like an undercover brother

A promise; give the best I can
even read for you on demand
Just ask, I'll appreciate and understand
Just place MY book in my hand

While on vacation, walking in the sand, dodging a tan 'cause I'm already tanned Sunglasses on, watching that muscle-man, perusing and searching as I scan that sand seeing if you've got my book in your hand. Get it for a friend – available now!

White Darkness   The question is the answer

What's a tree without the leaves?
How about the wind without the breeze?
An ice cube without the freeze?
Better yet, cheddar without the cheese?

    You ask – what is this poem all about?
    What is this chick really talking about?
    I'm merely talking about you and me
    If we were not here – where would we be?

        What good is bumble without the bee?
        Why have freedoms if you're still not free?
        What good is eyesight if you refuse to see?
        Why can't we love humanity; him, her and me?

Ever had a tea bag without the tea?
What kind of existence can an empty life be?
This peace of mind sounds empty to me
If that's your life should it matter to me?

    Ain't that the tail wagging the dog?
    Ain't that the lily pad jumping the frog?
    Ain't that the darkness blinding white fog?
    More like the slop consuming the hog?

Like a window without the glass
Like a lawn without the grass
Like making "A's" and still not pass
Like moving slowly while running fast

    Rings blinging on both your hands
    Reach out to help your fellow man
    Two nice carats on your ear
    When Jesus speaks is He crystal clear
    You can still hear?

Come now, let's get it together
Start treating each other better
No text or emails; write a love letter
Show kindness however, whenever forever

    Now that's the cat chasing the dog
    That's the running shoe without the jog
    That's your square dance without the clog
    You just signed on to my blog, blog, blog

                    PEACE, MS CYNTHIA

WORDS

MS CYNTHIA

Words care less about our style
it's whether we inspire
man, woman and child
not impressive
using useless babble
unfamiliar words learned
in a game of scrabble

Some words we only
choose to write
Others we may or may not
choose to recite
others we may just memorize
some words some might not recognize
because they're in disguise
some words some people just despise
and the writer may somewhat compromise
but never the artistry of his or her words

poems, poetry, rap or song
there really is no right or wrong
sonnets, rhythm, rhyme or verse
use words as a blessing, never a curse
riding high in a limo
never dead in a hearse
or they're just useless, buried words

never to be heard

old school, new school
still about the words
current or throwback
you still hear what you heard
"float like a butterfly, sting like a bee"
out in three like Muhammad Ali

Lava Java, Jazzy T's or Atlanta's One Tweezy
you, Common, Young Joc or Yung Jeezy
those Ying Yang boyz, whispering talking sleezy
me quoting Langston in an LA speak-easy
remembering Malcolm, Martin, Biggie or Tu-Peezy
the people are moved by the power of the words

words bring about peace or bring about war
words ask the questions:
"what the hell are you fighting for?
living for? sitting for? what are you willing
to stand up and cry for, or lay down and die for???"

words can even set you free
free to be who you want to be
a new you, not like him, her or me
free your mind, close your eyes
so you can really see

"close my eyes, so I can see what?"
sh-h-h, don't talk - listen to your gut

you'll see what you feel
with your eyes wide shut

words are used to criticize
words are used for telling lies
let the critics do their job
criticize, accuse, lie and blog
leaving only those interested
in a winter fog…of words

words from the wise are a useful tool
or misunderstood in the mind of a fool
rambling on, trying to sound cool
while drowning in a shallow pool of words

some rip the mic, swapping spit; talking sh-t
am I at a disadvantage 'cause
I can't grab meatballs or a hard stick?
as a chic, my thoughts on that are split
does that reflect my wit?
or that my wit is less quick?
'cause I won't call you a n-gger
and I can't squeeze the trigger on that
which obviously skeet-skeet-skeets out
foul, straight from the bowel words-s-s-s-s?

it's starting to sound like insanity
all of this gratuitous profanity
not empowering words like it used to be
spoken with authority and responsibility

remember KRS-one, The Roots and Chuck D?
how about School Daze –Spike Lee
"Wake up!" (Last Poets, you know it)

seems we're living in a world of restlessness
and wreckless-ness and unconscious-mess
I'd rather feed your mind with needed consciousness
while facing life's reality –
I'm just using words, don't be mad at me

whether I'm speaking prose to cons
or young brothers saying hoe's for fun
better yet, a little run-a-way
"baby please don't run. I know you need help,
let me get you some"
this word battle can be won, sometimes using
many words, sometimes just one – love

when asked about the words that inspire me
I'm reminded of the **Words** that set my spirit free
Words that have stood the test of time
Words of wisdom not necessarily words of rhyme
Words to refer to each and every time
when this world is really blowing my mind
stories, prophesies, the most deplorable crimes
punished and forgiven time after time
Chronicles, parables, prayers and psalms
revealing revelations stressing right from wrong
sermons, baptisms, hymnals and songs

Words from valleys low and mountains high
Words from fire and sky to you and I
Beatitudes; truths until the day you die
even then your family feels guilty to cry
they all know why
they knew - you knew
read it-spoke it and was true to
the power of **THE WORD** – ya heard?

Pull it together young'uns
We need you!

We're aware of the exec's games that's played
We also know you're trying to get paid
You have the power to change the stage
What an impact you will have made
for future rappers and rap's history page

                                        Ms Cynthia

IS SEEING OR FEELING BELIEVING?

Ms Cynthia

Questions:
>What do you see when you're not looking?
>What do you feel when all feelings are gone?
>What do you say when there are no words left?
>What do you cry when your wells have run dry?
>How do you love when you've given your all?
>How do you pray when you've asked for it all?
>What do you hear when there's only silence?

Bonus question

>What do you smell when there's no fragrance or aroma, and your taste for life has fallen flat and bland?

Possible
Answers:
>You see internally,
>when not looking outwardly,
>wondering where you've gone.
>You feel emptiness and helplessness
>seeking answers to where you went wrong

Your words are suffocating
screaming wildly inside
then weak and feeble as if
they've met their demise
You cry anguish and pain
when rivers of tears are all dried
It's impossible to love
If what you feel is denied

When you pray, be thankful
Be appreciative for it all
  The good, bad and indifferent
  It's all good, heed the call

When in silence, hear that inner voice
It will bring back the smell of success
It invites you to be your very best
The sweet taste of victory
snaps you back to your feet
The recovery is bitter sweet
yet meat enough to eat!

Now get back your zest - you passed this test!

Your inner self is stronger than you realize
LISTEN TO IT, LEARN FROM IT
AND
LIVE LIFE

FOR MEN ONLY

LADIES STEP AWAY FROM THE PAGE
MEN ONLY! THANKS

FOR MEN ONLY

To My Male Supporters,

I thank you so much for venturing into my books. I am very encouraged by your comments and I'm thankful you've taken the opportunity to see for yourselves that there's no male bashing here – no need to. I talk to women about making clear and responsible choices in their relationships.

I do, however, address issues that give guys a bad name – uncontrolled anger, Domestic Abuse, Sexual Violence as well as Cheaters, but to be fair, I talk about the female Cheaters as well; no one is exempt. I'm keeping it real.

I like that you are benefiting from some of my Love suggestions to the women. Just know guys, when she's happy, you're most likely to reap the benefits of her joy. So be smart and go that extra mile. Let her win that argument and turn off that TV while she's still alert so you can receive your rewards of love and passion. After all, you've exhibited all that understanding right? Guys, trust me on this, ok?

In all sincerity, I appreciate that you treat your woman respectfully. I'm sure you're that special kind of man, because if you weren't, you wouldn't be reading this. Just know that your woman is the envy of all her friends and if they're flirting with you, just smile and tell them how much you love your lady – They'll be even more impressed.

Men, take it from me – Women respect you more when you're strong enough and able to walk away from their advances. They're usually just trying to see what type of man their friend is involved with. If you think they're impressed by you coming on to them – they're not. They'll go back and tell your lady, sometimes after they've gotten the goods – your goods. And if it's not good, they'll tell that also. Trust me on that one; don't go there.

Some of you have asked me to write a book for men. My books are designed to enable everyone to have a better understanding of this thing called Love.

I've never been a man and doubt seriously if I'll ever be one, so the best I can do is speak from that which I know well; being a woman, one hell of one. And when I talk relationships, I speak from a common sense perspective that men and women surely are different, but we should all respect that. That's part of the fun!

The television has taken over teaching our kids things we should be displaying. Please show love in front of your children so they can learn from you - spiritual and respectful love, with hugs, kisses and kind words. Watch them smile and blush like its Christmas morning. They learn from us – don't let the TV parent your children. And believe this – every boy wants to be like his dad and every little girl is drawn to men like her father. Are you the example you envision in their lives later? It's not all on mom. Thanks guys, I'm betting on you.

Always With Love, Ms Cynthia
(P.S. read on. I've got a special treat for you)

FOR MEN ONLY
Methodology for Great Hanky Panky

Ms Cynthia

Sh-s-s-sh, don't tell the girls I gave away the secrets that will get her motor running and her temp up every time. This method operates on a ten point system, so guys, listen up …

O.K. men, I've got to make this quick, so listen with your hearts and not bull-headedness. This one's for you.

As difficult as you may think it is to keep your woman romantically aroused on a regular basis; it's actually quite simple. The tips I'm about to offer you are almost always fool proof. You must, however, be willing to follow these instructions to obtain the best results.

If you're one that likes to snuggle and kiss in the morning, take time to get up and freshen your face and breath, give her the opportunity to do the same, and oh, what a way to start your day! (Point 1)

Now first, understand that making love to a woman does not start in the bedroom at night. It can, however, be a great place for a wonderful ending. Making love to your love one starts as soon as you open your eyes every morning. Not clawing and digging at her while she's trying to get herself and the kids off for the day, but by simply acknowledging her with kind comments and assistance with the kids would help greatly. (2)

As she's leaving out the door, all hurried and not quite sure if her appearance is what it should be, or if her hair is not behaving as she'd like – a simple word of encouragement or anything positive from you will at least bring her some calm. You don't have to lie about the outfit or the hair – just find something nice to say – "love ya' babe, have a nice day" is usually sufficient if you find you're lost for words. Smile and move on unless her body language says she could use a hug. (*3 points already*)

During the course of the day, if your job allows and her does too, give your lady a call and say something sweet. No, not "what ya' cookin tonite honey?" *or even "what ya' cookin sweet tonight?" Not cute. A simple "I was thinking about you and wanted to hear your voice. Gotta get back to the grind, see ya' tonight."* (you're up to 4)

I know what some of you are thinking right now. "My wife is going to think I'm up to something if I start doing and saying of this all of a sudden." And you're absolutely right. As simple as these things are to do, ask yourself why haven't you been doing them all along. Doesn't cost you a thing to be a little more sincere and attentive. And believe me, the rewards – worth it! OK, we're up to four points and it's only lunch time. You're doing great.

Now, Once you get home, whether she's home or not, start looking around to see if there's anything you can do to cut down on some of her chore time. Please, don't wait for her to ask. Take out the trash, clean the commode, after all, you see under the seat more often than she does. And guys please, don't make a mess cleaning

up a mess. Heard that before huh? Its ok, we love you. Anything worth doing is worth doing right, and half doing something is not better than doing nothing at all. Simply ask her if there's anything in particular she needs you to do. If she starts rattling off a long list of overdue repairs and things she's been asking you to do for the last five years – **breathe** – then calmly say " I hear you baby, don't blow this for me, I'm trying to make an improvement here. Is there anything specific you need me to do n-o-ow?"
No matter how she responds, out of her own frustration, don't let it get to you. Assist her or don't, but don't lose your cool. She will feel she owes you because you were trying. That didn't make you a wimp – that gave you *Point 5 and 6*

OK, it's getting later in the evening - you're in good shape. She's starting to wind down after dinner so this is a great time to double up on your points. Ask yourself, did you offer to get dinner, make dinner, or at least comment favorably about the meal? Now you can help clean the kitchen or place the dishes in the dishwasher or whatever method your home uses. Be sure to keep your voice calm and soothing throughout the evening. It wouldn't hurt to ask about her day and don't criticize anything – even if she's been complaining about the same things since she's been on that job, just nod. You'd be surprised how much her venting will relieve her stress though it seems to be increasing it. So you're up to 7 or 8 points by now.

The big test is now headed your way 90 mph – the phone calls from well meaning girlfriends. Yeah, gossip and all, just be patient. Go ahead and get your shower out of the way – easy on the cologne.

And know, whether tonight works out or not, the points are in the bank drawing interest – no pressure ok? *Point 9*

She's probably noticing by now that you're seriously trying to understand her as a woman. Not just your "baby's mama", your cook, cleaner, driver, washwoman, and object of sexual pleasure. In fact, if you only cuddle the first night of this new you – an automatic 5 extra points. Unless she initiates and then… well… you know, go for it!

You're at the end of the evening, your television shows are on in separate rooms, and awkwardness rears it's head. Should you sacrifice everything you enjoy just to spend intimate time with your love one? Surely, you can watch the game and she should stay awake to show you her appreciation for all your efforts. How long can you keep up this new you? And what if she still doesn't respond the way you would like her to?

Only you can answer those questions. What is it worth to you? God has blessed you with a gift. How much is too much for you to go through to see a smile on her face? How much will it take for some of you to understand that name calling, putdowns and references like **stupid, bitch** and **whore** are not going to be forgotten or forgiven when it's bedtime and you're feeling frisky. Don't wonder why she's not – think about it. Also, don't ever think that the five c's are an adequate substitute for loving kindness and affection. The five c's? You know - cash, cars, carats, clothes and credit cards. Try placing more emphasis on your relationship and those things that are solid that will stand the test of time. Then the gifts and trinkets are so much more meaningful. Now don't misunderstand; they are great additions to the relationship and will bring smiles of joy. The five c's partnered with your love and respect for her – priceless.

What would it mean to you to have her look at you admirably and smile, thanking God for her wonderful husband; one that supports her hopes, dreams and accomplishments with encouragement and a sense of pride for his bride.

So, the ball is in your court. You decide if that last point is worth it to you. If the games, that last sometimes into the early morning, or hanging out with your friends at the clubs and bars, offer something more important than building your relationship at home, don't worry about the points. They will only be redeemed with animosity. But if you can rethink what's really important to you and make a commitment to being more loving and considerate – What are you waiting for? You've got a steaming perfect ten waiting for you. Turn off that TV and go score some points for yourself. In fact, try to work on some extra innings or an overtime game. Warm oil massages are great for warm ups. Three pointers, home runs, touch downs and slam dunks are all welcomed. And please go for the hole-in-one, that's always a winner.

Nite-nite and Happy Hanky Panky to ya'

Can't wait to hear from you   tomscynthia@gmail.com

Ladies a Mega Shout Out to: The Men who Love Us

Cynthia

As quiet as it's kept, there are quite a few men out there who are simply wonderful. They are actually everything the little girl's story books spoke about; our heroes. They are handsome, kind, thoughtful, helpful and they know how to treat a woman; not beat a woman.

You might say, "If they're handsome, they're certain not to be kind or thoughtful". I beg to differ with you. I have met couples, since writing these books that have shared much inside info with me. I've met men that were so polite, caring and, sincerely' in love with their ladies, it brought joy to my heart. You know I had to ask these sisters in private, "girl, is he really like this or is he fronting for me? I knew, before she answered by the look on her face, she had found a real man. The glow these women show speak louder about the relationship than anything they could say. The 'woman glow' is a tale- tale sign that something is going very well.

Another news flash – all men don't cheat. The single divas informed me of this. As sad as it was for them to admit, some ladies actually prefer married men, but all men are not up for it. These divas walked away knowing that there's still a chance for true love and happiness after all.

Now we are all aware of the situations out there that cause women to tremble with fear when they dare think of a relationship, but let's be honest, we know it's not all men.

Some men are indeed dangerous and they don't wear signs but they show signs long before. We need to be more aware. There are always signs – learn to read them.

So to all you sisters out there who have a man that brings you flowers or a single flower for no reason, even if it's from your own yard and hidden behind his back- be thankful

If you have a man that encourages you and tells you you're still the sexiest thing he's seen lately, knowing time is taking a toll on your body and mind, and he just saw Beyonce and Shakira on the video, he walks up and grabs you like he did years ago, its ok - be thankful

If your man buys you gifts and surprises you often with just the little things saying "baby this reminded me of you, or I thought you might like this"– be thankful

If your man calls just to say "I love you baby" and that makes his day and yours – be thankful

If your man does 50 things well and you complain about the one he didn't do as well and he still loves you and tries to get that one thing down pat – be thankful

If your man washes your car, vacuums the inside and fills your gas tank without mentioning a word – be thankful

If your man buys you outfits, knowing he's never seen you in the ones he bought before hoping one day you'll like what he's chosen – be thankful

If your man cooks you meals, though he's not the best cook and you can taste the love – be thankful

If your man cleans up the kitchen, putting everything away after you've finished the meal – be very thankful

If he volunteers to wash or rub your back even when your day wasn't so hard – be thankful

If he ask if you'd like a foot massage knowing you've had a hard day and you say "no" and he then ask if there's anything he can do to help you feel more comfortable – be thankful

If your man plans quaint little get-a-ways and you never want to get away because of other obligations, and he asks instead what you'd like to do – be thankful

If your man is not intimidated by you watching Oprah and actually watches with you and ask about your views on the subject matter – that's not gay, that's a man . Be thankful

If your man compliments you on your way out to meet your girlfriends for Girls Nite Out, and tells you how sexy you look and that he and his will be waiting up for you – be thankful

If your man is a hard worker, or doesn't have to work hard, but pays the bills, is thrifty, works in the yard and goes out of his way to make sure your needs are met – be thankful

If your man helps clean house, wash and fold clothes, helps the kids with homework, ask you about your day, runs you a bubble bath, insist the kids give you your private time to unwind, listens to your suggestions, tells you your meals are better than his moms, and consistently tries to improve on his love making skills just for your pleasure …
Thank GOD for blessing you with a wonderful man, tell those kids "lights out" and mean it!
And **Girlfriend, put this book down and go handle your business!**

Remember: Always reward the good. You can get back to this later. Have fun

SISTER STRENGTH

PEARLS FOR MY GIRLS

From Ms Cynthia with love

Valuable gifts from me to you
By all means cash them in

Knowledge is learned
Wisdom is earned
And we have the mental and physical
scars to prove it

A girl in need, needs a girlfriend indeed

Never place the gift before the giver
Especially when it's Jesus
"The lord giveth …

Learn, live and love
for the rest of your life
Or until you die; whichever comes first

Don't use sorry to the point that
It becomes who you are
rather than What you say

The easiest way to avoid repeating
Gossip is to refuse to listen to it

good ol' common sense

will dictate that you stop
trying To make sense of nonsense

Age doesn't age you;
not bothering to care For yourself does

If your man is sexually involved With another woman
So are you; Just not by choice
So, if you're going to mix DNA with this woman
why not Cut out the middle man?
(Sisters, condoms please!)
what goes up
needs to stay up
at least until she's done

if she took your man
Press charges and name the weapon
It's illegal to steal
But if he left to be with her
Sorry, case dismissed
You may step down

Just because your man doesn't find you sexy
Don't take it personally, you probably are
It's not necessarily another woman
Maybe it's another man

one of the original divas –
MS MAE WEST
"A good man is hard to find
And
A hard man is good to find"

Now Ladies, listen up,
I know it gets hard sometime – if you're lucky Just kidding
But seriously, when trying to make that choice
Between right and wrong
Weak or strong
Just ask yourself
"Would I be OK if he did it? (Probably not)

or

"Chances are I won't get caught
but if I do
can I wear the consequences? (Probably not)
and
is it worth it? am I willing to risk losing what/who I have
(only you know that answer)
if you're still struggling, put this last one first

A no brainer
"What would Jesus do?"
don't worry about us - know he's watching you

My first book, "To My Sisters with Love" extended thanks to the trailblazers from the past as well as sisters of today. I continue that list with these outstanding ladies.

THANK YOU SISTERS

Your strength and drive have propelled you to greatness. We are encouraged by your tenacity and further empowered by your accomplishments. May you be blessed as you continue to strive for excellence in your own unique way.

JADA   *BEYONCE*   WHOPPI   *ELLEN*   MADONNA   *WHITNEY*
MARIAH   VENUS   SERENA
HALLE   *TYRA*   INDIA   *VIVICA*   NIA   MARY J
ANGELINA   MONIQUE   *GABRIEL*   STAR   *JOSS*   CELINE
MICHELLE Obama, Williams   KATIE Couric   MARY Hart   NANCY Pelosi
HILLARY Clinton   PAULA Deen   ANGELA Bassett, Winbush
JILL Scott   DEBBIE Morgan   LESLIE Stahl   QUEEN LATIFAH
JENNIFER Lopez, Hudson, Anniston   ANNIE Lennox   GWEN Ifill
LINDA Johnson   CHERYL Crow, Underwood, Swoops, Lee-Ralph
CATHY Hughes   CAROL King   ANN Curry   TINA Marie
PEARL Cleage   J K Rowling   CONDI Rice   Dr JOHNETTA Cole
PAULETTA Washington   ROBIN Roberts, Givens   DAPHNE Reid
JANET Jackson   KELLY Ripa, Rowland, Clarkston   ANGIE Stone
MARTINA Mcbride, Hingis, Navratilova   DEBORAH Roberts, Lee, Norville
MERIDITH Vieira   KATHY Lee   KIMORA Lee   WENDY Williams
TRACY Ross, Edmonds   VICTORIA Rowell, Principal   JULIA Roberts
RACHAEL Ray, Hunter   CHANDRA Wilson   ALICIA Keys, Silverstone
Characters: MADEA *-*MARGE SIMPSON *-* BIONIC WOMAN *-* JESSICA RABBIT
SUSAN G. KOMEN *FOR THE CURE*

YOU LOVE ME? I CAN'T TELL

Ms Cynthia

You love me, but you're not N love with me
Oh no, not that tired ass line again
I don't blame you, I blame me
You see, I loved you to the point that each time I allowed
you to discount, embarrass or humiliate me
I gave up another piece of myself
I gave up that part of me I'm suppose to hold in esteem
Yeah, self esteem
The self I no longer hold in esteem because I lowered
myself to be taken for granted, misused and neglected
I gave you permission to do all of those things
when I said nothing
I was actually saying "It's OK to treat me this way".
That was 'my bad' not yours

I even thought that cooking all those fine meals
and having our children would be something you
would adore me for, but seems you now abhor me for.
Yes, the foxy diva you married now has a pouch, cellulite,
extra pounds and even thinning hair. Guess what Big Papa
so do you!

Being neglected in a negligee has got to be one of the
most dreadful occurrences a woman can ever experience
I'm fully aware that I don't have the body of a well built

twenty five year old; nor should you expect me to.
I expect you to still be N Love with me and this body and
not let me down simply because gravity has

I'm sure those younger women
make you feel like a younger, more virile man
but look in the mirror honey
The hip-hop clothing and overpriced sneakers
didn't peel away the years; just your sense of who
you really are

I have to admit though
I only wish I felt as good about myself as you do
Maybe you feel so good about you
because I was N love with you and showed it
I always wanted you to be confident – and you are
So now I get it! I just need to love myself like that,
actually, even more, and feed my own self confidence

I gave good love, great love and didn't save any for me
I thought I needed your love to survive
I needed mine
I needed to love me especially when you didn't
And as much as this hurts, I'll admit it
If I had loved myself more
you probably would have too
and even found me irresistible
Even if you didn't or don't ever, it's OK
Because, believe me, someone will be *N love* with the new me
even if it's only me

THE LOVE YOURSELF CHALLENGE

MS CYNTHIA

- Hug yourself – now hold you for awhile
- Look in the mirror at yourself and smile
- Take a nice long walk, at least a mile
- Now hug and love a hurting child

- Remove old nail color; give those nails a file
- Clean that closet, wash those items; at least one pile
- Think of an elderly person – pick up that phone and dial
- Write a letter to your congressman and tell him you're riled

- Write out that ten percent and walk it down that aisle
- Buy yourself a new outfit that has lots of style
- Find yourself a dance floor; wood, linoleum or tile
- And dance, dance, dance girl, free your spirit – dance buck wild

Mrs. Irene –
She lives next door to herself

Ms Cynthia

Looking back... She came up in South Carolina
The low country, A native accent, AND who could be finer?
Her love, the one who happened to find her
His name was Joseph

I asked her "tell me a little about your life?"
She spoke of her struggles, toil and strife
She spoke of her children
Then smiled about being Joe's wife

She'd moved to be with the one she loved
They moved only one state above
Moving to Highpoint would be her high
His love was all she needed to get her by
Then...
Why did her sweet, sweet Joe have to die?
Her soul cried "why? Dear Lord tell me why
Did you need my sweet Joe in the sweet by and by?"

She spoke of him candidly through salty tears
She smiled saying "he gave me ten sweet years,
                  A boy and some girls" spoke this lady
"And when he died, I was pregnant with Joe's baby,
He told me it was a boy, Oh, Joe's baby!"

Her highs in Highpoint soon became her low
Back to the low country where she buried her Joe
Back to Georgetown she and her children did go
Was her survival questioned? Probably so

Little mouths to feed
and pregnant
Her husband deceased
No doubt her troubles would soon increase
Her back strong, head high, not sure what she'd do
She prayed to God and talked to Joe
"I know the **lord** will see us through"

The possibility of another husband?
She shook her head no
No way and no how would there be another Joe
A few men came but soon they'd go
They knew it was impossible to replace her Joe
Yet, room in her heart for two more sons though

I asked her
"Anything else in your life you'd like to share?"
She looked at me as if to ask "why do you care?"
Through her saddened eyes I sensed her despair
Her heart spoke to me clearly "It wasn't fair"

She's the mother of eight - four boys and four girls
gathered around their mother's neck
her precious strand of pearls
Her children are educated, accomplished

Their families all living quite well
How you ask?
Prayers and secrets she'll never tell

Next door are her church hats,
and old memories on the shelf
Oh Joe's baby?
He bought his mama a new home
next door to herself
In her new home are family photos
a generation she's proud to show
also pictures of her and Joe
taken over fifty years ago
Joe in his army uniform
sitting uniformly by himself
Sweet, sweet memories
so much more than wealth
Him smiling at his lady,
"I WAS ALWAYS WITH you baby"
She smiles back, "I know Joe"
keeping that secret to herself

FIFTY/50 LOVE

Ms Cynthia

So tell me, what's with this 50/50 love?
Is it 50% of you will be there 50% of the time?
The other 50% is what? Where?
And why I would want 50% of anything
I really want???

Is your love like very expensive wine
served in a half-full wine goblet
large and clear enough to swirl, swish and spit,
while measuring your tear factor which will therefore
reveal your true quality to me? Sorry, I'm not that deep

You say you love me *'so much'*.
'So much' means ½ as much as what?

I'm afraid if we meet only halfway
and I happen to lose my way,
you won't be willing to travel that other half
in order for us to meet and continue to complete
our journey into oneness

Said you would cry for me
damn-near die for me
Are you going to cry from one eye
and half-ass die
only to be resuscitated?

You "care and will always be there" for me
I half understand that since you probably care from
the left half where your heart lives. But, I'm half concerned
if the right brain will care for me while I'm out on the
left hanging out with your heart? Mind boggling isn't it?

I asked all of that to simply say this-
Please, don't love me, leave me or meet me half way
I am 100% woman
Rather than existing in halves
I can live totally - give my all - and still be 100%
I am 100% complete by myself; I really can't use 50%
If you're only offering 50% to this relationship
you're holding onto 50% for yourself - if that's so,
why do you need me? You've already got yourself covered,
if only half way – just in case.

When you figure out how to give all to this relationship, call me.
I don't want or need ½ a man, at least not now.
But you never know,
I just might need that rib one day and, hey, I'll give you a call.
"Can you help a sister out?"

When you're ready to bring that half that lives in fear,
hiding and waiting until this half you offer falters,
I'd really like to meet him and introduce him
to a whole woman who believes-
Giving all is the only way to survive love.

I thank you for the offer,
but I don't care to be your other half
better half, lower or upper half
With Christ, I'm whole and I wish the same for you
I'll give you all or none of me
while holding onto all of me
If you come back, bring all of you and be willing to
hold onto you and me too as the two become one
Is that math too fuzzy for you? Simply put:
All or nothing at all

50 in a 100 world = half, almost, a ways to go, middle, failing
100 + 100 = 200 (surplus)   200 over 200 = 1

"HEY, I CAN DO THE SAME MATH WITH 50/50"

"GREAT, DO IT WITHOUT ME"

half empty, half full – Who cares
half way there – so what, call me when you get there
half is better than none – only for those who settle

OH NOTHIN' HONEY, JUST TALKIN TO MYSELF

MS CYNTHIA

"Hey honey, there's not a single slice of bread in this house."
Well there would be if you didn't stay up making yourself late night snacks and leaving a mess every chance you get.
"What?"
"Did you know this trash smells really bad, ya' think something's spoiled?"
I'm sure of it. I just wanted to see if you would finally take it out without being asked.
"Huh?"
"Baby, guess what, my pin striped shirt is wrinkled and I need to wear it tomorrow.
I guess you'll be looking tacky at work because I'm tired; learn how to iron.
"Are you saying something, I can't hear you?"
"Honey, can you lend me twenty dollars for gas, I forgot to stop by the ATM?"
You always forget to stop by the ATM, maybe because you're overdrawn again.
"Are you talking to me or who?" *Why are you mumbling?*
"Anyway, listen, can you pick up my suits from the dry cleaners since I don't have any cash on me."
Not only do you not have any cash on you, you also don't have any anywhere else either. The games you play are really starting to sicken me.

"Sweetheart, it would be great if you cooked us breakfast in the morning, you know, the most important meal of the day. We should start the day off right."

We sure will, those frozen sausage biscuits will get us right off in one minute or less.

"Why aren't you answering me baby? Don't you hear me talking to you?"

Sure I do honey, I was in meditation and praying for God to give me strength,

patience and a willing spirit to deal with those that tend to abuse our good nature.

You understand that don't you dear?

"Oh yeah baby, I told you long time ago that your friends would try to use you. You've got to be firm and let people know where you stand. Don't let 'em run over you."

Yeah, yeah, it's always somebody else. You're right, I need to stand up to you more.

"What did you say, why do you seem to be whispering?"

Oh nothing honey, just talking to myself.

"Well, you need to stop that. My mama used to do that – my old man said that's the first sign to look out for – when a woman starts talking to herself. Oh hell! You're

not about to leave me are you? Aren't you happy? I'm gonna do better, I promise.

YOUNG GIRLS ADMIRATION

MS CYNTHIA

I WATCHED ANXIOUSLY AS YOU ENTERED THE ROOM
YOU WALKED WITH SO MUCH CONFIDENCE
I KNEW RIGHT THEN AND THERE
I WANTED TO BE JUST LIKE YOU WHEN I GREW UP
THE PEOPLE IN THE ROOM SEEMED UNCOMFORTABLE
THEY SEEMED AS NERVOUS AS I WAS BY YOUR PRESCENCE
I LIKED THAT. I SAID TO MYSELF "SOMEDAY I'M GOING
TO COMMAND A ROOM JUST LIKE THAT – JUST LIKE YOU

I SAT UP AND LISTENED TO THE WAY YOU SPOKE
YOUR WORDS WERE SO CLEAR.
YOU SOUNDED AS IF YOU COULD BE ON TV
YOUR VOICE WAS LIKE MUSIC
IT FLOWED AND SOUNDED LIKE IT WAS SMILING
EVEYONE WAS SMILING AS YOU ARTICULATED EVEN
SIMPLE WORDS WE HEAR EVERYDAY
YES, ONE DAY THAT'S GOING TO BE ME – EXACTLY LIKE YOU

I COULD REALLY APPRECIATE YOUR STYLE
YOUR CHOICE OF CLOTHING WAS JUST RIGHT
THE JUST RIGHT COLOR, FIT AND LENGTH
I WANT TO LOOK PROFESSIONAL
WHEN IT'S MY TURN TO SPEAK BEFORE PEOPLE
I WANT TO MAKE THEM SMILE AND SIT UP JUST LIKE YOU

I NOTICED EVERYTHING ABOUT YOU.

I LOOK AT YOUR NAILS, YOUR NEATLY STYLED HAIR,
YOUR CLEAN SHAVEN LEGS, EVEN YOUR SHOES WERE JUST RIGHT
YOUR EARRINGS AND ACCESSORIES WERE EXACTLY AS THEY SHOULD BE
I EVEN SAW HOW YOUR MAKUP WAS DISTRIBUTED EVENLY THE COLORS BLENDED SO WELL
YOUR LIPSTICK LOOKED SO BRILLIANT BECAUSE YOUR TEETH WERE SO BRIGHT
LIKE I SAID, I NOTICED EVERYTHING – YOU WERE POLISHED
I KNOW NOW, THIS IS HOW I WANT TO BE

YOUR WALK, YOUR STANCE AND EVEN YOUR MANNERISMS SCREAMED "CHARISMA AND INTEGRITY" I WAS SO EXCITED
I COULDN'T WAIT TO MEET YOU.
WHEN I SAW YOU COMING TOWARD ME, I STEPPED OUT SO YOU COULD NOTICE ME,
AND YOU DID AND SMILED
I JUST KNEW I WAS GOING TO FAINT WHEN YOU STARTED WALKING TOWARD ME
YOU SMILED AND SAID "HI". OH MY GOD, YOU HUGGED ME
I NEVER SMELLED ANYBODY OR ANYTHING SO FRAGRANT.

I WANTED TO ASK YOU A MILLION QUESTIONS LIKE-
ARE THOSE YOUR REAL LASHES? DID YOU WEAR BRACES?
ARE THOSE YOUR REAL NAILS? WHO CUTS YOUR HAIR?

WHERE DID YOU GO TO COLLEGE? WHAT DID YOU STUDY?
WAS IT REALLY HARD? WHAT'S THAT PERFUME? CAN I
EMAIL YOU?
BUT I WAS TOO OVERWHELMED BY YOUR BEAUTY

I FOLLOWED YOU AS YOU WALKED OUTSIDE AND I HEARD
YOU TALKING TO
SOMEONE YOU KNEW FROM CHILDHOOD. SHE WAS
CONGRATULATING
YOU ON YOUR ACCOMPLISHMENTS AND YOU SMILED, SHE
SMILED AND I WAS
SMILING TOO. THEN I HEARD HER CURSE AND SAY
SOMETHING REALLY FOUL
I HEARD YOU RESPOND BACK TO HER THE SAME WAY; YOU
BOTH LAUGHED.
ALL MY DREAMS OF BEING JUST LIKE YOU CAME CRASHING
DOWN
YOU ARE NO LONGER BEAUTIFUL TO ME AND I WILL NEVER
TALK LIKE THAT.
NOW I'M SO DISAPPOINTED - I DON'T KNOW ANY MORE
ROLE MODELS
BE CAREFUL WHAT YOU SAY AND WHAT YOU DO- YOU NEVER KNOW WHO'S IMPRESSED BY YOU

Feature Story

THE SWEETEST THING THAT NEVER HAPPENED

MS CYNTHIA
CO-AUTHOR   NAPOLEON CURTAIN

THE SWEETEST THING THAT NEVER HAPPENED

MS CYNTHIA
Co author – NAP CURTAIN

Friday Night 9:12pm

Yeah girl, I know you told me so, but I just didn't want to believe it. I just couldn't make myself believe that it would end this way. For three and a half years he's been consistently proving you and all the nay sayers wrong. I could count on this man for anything, anytime, no matter what. He was so precious, considerate and prompt. You would think his heartbeat was a golden time piece.

You called it girl, all good things must come to an end, but I swear, I didn't see this one coming. Just in the last six months, he's been working late, tired and preoccupied all the time, even whispering on the phone. You know all the usual signs. At first, I thought I was just being paranoid, but lately it had gotten worse. I asked him calmly, straight up, "what is up with this sudden change in our relationship?" He just smiled, hugged me close and said "What baby? If anything, I love you more than ever". Now that's a cold way to set somebody up if you plan on dropping them. I wonder if it's because my credit wasn't approved for the house I was trying to buy? I just knew I had cleaned everything up but when they asked me to come in, sign, and finalize everything, they called me back and said that there had been a mistake. I guess he realized then that he didn't want a woman with a poor credit rating. How would he be able to improve his life while dragging along dead weight that couldn't even get credit approval?

Like tonight, we were supposed to be on a date. We were going to talk things out and really get to the bottom line. Like I was saying, this is a man that's never late and if he thought he was going to be, he would call and let me know. He was always considerate like that. But tonight he's fifteen minutes late and hasn't bothered to call. I pray nothings wrong, but after the way he's been acting, I seriously doubt it.

Another thing I need to know – who is Lunnie? The other day I was at his apartment and the phone rang. I didn't dare answer it because we respect each other that way, or we did before all of this bullshit started. Anyway, the answering machine picked up and I hear this jovial voice " hellooo, this is Lun-neee and I have e-ve-ry thing you need. Call me, same number on the card I gave you. Look forward to hearing from you – it's going to be a blast! I can't wait. Smooches!"

I thought "What!" I know this man cannot be on the 'down low' and I not know! I couldn't tell anybody and I couldn't ask him because,well you know, we trust each other.

I wish to hell I hadn't been there to hear that message. It would have hurt to find out that he had another woman but a MAN! I just can't deal with all of this. I'm really so hurt and confused right now. I should have listened to you girl and not even gotten involved with somebody too good to be true. I thought you were just jealous- I admit it. I need to think and pray and breathe my way through this one. I know he'll be trying to call me when he snaps back to reality or finishes whatever he's doing with his new

Romeo lover or whatever. So I'm hanging up now and I'm turning off my ringer. I'm going to put my cell phone on my car charger and I'll talk to you sometime later tomorrow. I don't want to be tempted to listen to some weak bullshit about where he was and why he's just now calling. This is so not like him, I'm telling you. Well he can have Lunnie and ram him up his a.., but then, he'd like that wouldn't he? I'm so damn mad I'm stupid. Thank you for letting me vent girl, bye.

Saturday morning 9:00am

I can't sleep. I might as well get up and check my phone. I need to know that this relationship was not all just a game. Let me turn my phones back on to see what type of lies he's left for me. I still love him and to tell the truth I want to hear his voice. Why did he have to mess things up? I can't believe he didn't try to come over when he couldn't reach me. Lunnie must be some kind'a honey. Boy bitch!

Hmm, only two missed calls, one message. I can't wait to hear this. Any other time he would have left at least five or six messages to make sure I was OK when he couldn't reach me. That's odd; these are strange numbers, it's not even him. I don't feel like talking to anyone so whoever left these messages can wait until Monday or whenever. Damn, I just can't believe this. How could anyone change like this overnight? I really thought he was different - he was actually more different than I thought.

Ding dong, ding dong

Oh, so he thinks he can just run his ass over here without clearance? He must be tripping. Let me get this door and cuss his ass completely out! Oh, hi, may I help you officers? Is there something wrong? Yes, I am. What do you mean? What are you saying? No! Oh God no, I don't believe you, you're lying to me – what? NO-oooooooooooooooooooooooo …

"Ma'am, there was an accident last evening. There were some teenagers playing truth or dare on the highway and they were driving on the wrong side directly into oncoming traffic. When we got to him, he was barely conscious. He asked us to contact you but we were unable to reach you at that time and we couldn't leave a voice message with this type of information—sorry. Ma'am, we realize this is not a good time but really, there never is. When you're able to pull yourself together, there were some things in his car he wanted you to have. He made us promise to get these things to you before they crush the car. The car is already practically crushed anyway. It's a miracle he was alive when we arrived on the scene. Ma'am, honestly we understand how difficult this has to be right now, but you must come and claim the property now so they can continue with this investigation – please. We'll give you a little more time to get yourself together."

What do you mean claim? Claim the property? Is he dead? What exactly are you saying? I know you said he was in an accident and barely conscious, but are you telling me he didn't make it? Oh my God, this is too much. I can't do this right now – I can't do this at all!
"Ma'am if you would just come with us. We can help you to find out that information, we don't know. We're just here to keep our

promise to him to get those items to you. We can't bring them because you will need to sign off on all of the items you remove from his vehicle. Ma'am we can phone the hospital to find out his condition. I'm sure they probably tried to phone you last night as well. He was adamant about reaching you. In fact, in the ambulance, he was struggling to use his cell phone to call you himself. They had to take it away because of the oxygen tank and they knew he was in too bad of a condition to be trying to talk. Is there anyone else that we should contact? He only gave us your number and address."

So you're saying that you think he's alright? Well I don't mean alright, but he's going to be OK? "Ma'am we're not saying anything because we really don't know at this point. We've seen people make it through worse, but to be honest, most don't – we don't want to give you false hope, it was pretty bad. So can you leave with us now and we can find out?"

No, let me call the hospital first and then we can go.

Ring, ring, ring

OK, wait, let me get the phone. Maybe that's him. He can tell me what he wants me to do. Hold on. Hello – this is who? Lunee's Restaurant? Yes I am.

"Madame, I'm just phoning to see why your reservations were not cancelled on last evening? We went to all the trouble to do everything your fiancé requested and it was such a waste! A waste I tell you!"

"I have tried several times to phone him but to no avail. I was hopeful that the two of you might be there together so we can straighten out this travesty. I know it was suppose to be a surprise, but since you didn't show up last evening, I'm sure I'm not giving anything away".

Sir, I have no idea what you're rambling on about and he's not here.

"Oh honey, did he run out on you? I simply can not believe that. He pre-paid for everything and was so excited that I just wanted to see why such a perfectly planned evening was thrown away. He was intent on making this one of the grandest evenings ever and I couldn't wait to meet the lucky woman who deserved all he had gone through to create this magical evening. So what happened girl, if you don't mind my asking? Dish the dirt honey."

Sir, I can't right now. We'll get back with you later.

"But you don't understand. Let me explain to you all he had me go through. He'd arranged a dining experience with all the trimmings that you would never forget. He ordered two bottles of our finest champagne and special ordered flutes with your names engraved in platinum trim. He said you adored harp and violin music, so we hired the very best this city had to offer just for your private table in our finest dining room. We had enough roses, rose petals and candles everywhere to blow you away as you entered the doorway. And to top it off girl, we were to release three dozen white doves when he proposed to you on the veranda after dessert, after you said yes, of course, and after all that, why wouldn't you? At any rate, everyone here was disappointed to say the least. We simply couldn't imagine or figure out why you would ruin our entire evening even if you messed up yours! A simple call ahead of time would have been nice don't you think? Is that too much to ask -a little thing called common courtesy?"

We'll have to c…I'll have him ca… I'm going to have to get with you later on this, bye. What is all of this about? Fiancé, white doves, Lunee's Restaurant?

"Ma'am, was that the hospital? If not we really need to leave now. We've got to finish this paperwork and have what's left of his car towed. Ma'am, are you alright? Who was on the phone?" Lonnie, I mean Lunee. He's the owner of Lunee's Restaurant.
"Lunee's? That's a first class place. Is that where you guys were heading last evening? Your fiancé sure was dressed to impress. We figured he must'a been headed somewhere really nice. Such a shame those kids ruined your evening playing around. They didn't even get hurt. In fact they phoned the accident in. Said they were just trying to scare drivers off the road. The other couple involved in the accident didn't make it. Not only did they ruin your evening, they ruined lives. Are you ready?" I guess so, might as well.

Ring, ring, ring

"Ma'am, could you cut this call short? We really need to get going". OK, ok, in fact, could you get that for me? I don't think I can take anymore. If it's good news let me have it, if it's nothing I can get back to them later. I'm starting to feel nauseous and confused.
So much is happening. No, wait, maybe it's him. Let me get it. I don't want him wondering what man is answering my phone after he couldn't reach me all night, wait… what? He hung up? Did you tell him you were a police officer? I told you to wait and not answer my damn phone! Why didn't you let me speak to him? I'll call back.
"Ma'am, that was the hospital. They just called to inform you that

he didn't make it. I'm so sorry. Is there anyone we can call to be with you right now, a family member, a friend, anyone?"

Oh God no! No, there's absolutely no one. Why did you take him Lord? Please tell me why, oh Lord why? Oh, what am I going to do? He was my best and only friend, not just my lover. Oh baby, you really did love me and I blew my only chance to speak to you for the last time. Oh God, how will I ever forgive myself? Help me make sense of it all – I can't take this, help me!

Nobody understood me the way he did. My entire life has changed in just a matter of hours, how could this happen to me, my life, why me? "Ma'am we're leaving now. You can get those things later. We'll put things on hold for now. Just sign this giving us permission to collect the items and bring them to you. This is out of the ordinary but this is not an ordinary situation. Again, our condolences and call us when you're ready".

I won't be calling you. You can go ahead and have the car towed. "But ma'am, they're going to crush the car immediately if you don't claim the items." They could never crush that car more than my heart is this very minute.

I don't want to see or hear mention of those things again. They would only mean something to me if he was the one presenting them to me. The meaning behind whatever's in that car, died when he did. Crush the car.

"Yes ma'am. We'll tear this sheet up and give it to you and if you would sign this one giving permission to crush the vehicle. We're leaving now, is there anything else we can get you?"

No, just close and lock the door when you leave. Thank you for everything. I'm tired; I'm going to try to rest. Good bye.

"Ma'am, we're pretty sure you're in shock right now, I suggest you call someone to be with you. Maybe they can get the doctor to prescribe you something to help you through this ordeal. You're just a little too calm, please call someone".

OK, pass me my cell phone – I'll phone my girl Dee and my physician and have him call me in something. Don't forget to lock the door on you way out, please leave now. Thank you.

Oh baby, I'm so sorry I didn't trust you. I had no reason to doubt you. If I had only listened to my heart instead of negative interference, I wouldn't be crying my heart out now. It wouldn't have affected the accident, but my conscious would be clear. I feel as if I helped them kill you baby, please forgive me for not being there for you like you've always been there for me. If only I'd been there to love and pray you through, maybe this would have all turned out differently, I'll never know.

I guess now is a good a time as any to listen to this message. I'm sure it's from the hospital last night. I was too selfish to see that I honestly did have a good man and they were trying to reach me when he really needed me to be there.

Here we go - **messages, send, "You have one new message, to hear your messages please enter your pass word then press pound."**

She listens to the weak voice struggling to speak
Hey baby, it's me. So sorry I'm late; that's supposed to be a joke.
Baby I was in a car accident and I'm in the hospital. It sure would make me feel a lot better if you were here. I know you're looking so beautiful; dressed for our special date. I promise I'll make it up to you. Anyway, (cough, cough) since the date will be delayed somewhat, I need to first tell you how much I love you. I also have a confession (cough).

157

I sabotaged the deal on your house. I knew how much you loved it and I wanted to be the one to buy it for you; for us. Yes I purchased our new house. I had planned for us to celebrate tonight. Speaking of which, I need you to phone Lunee's Restaurant and cancel our reservations, I'll explain later. We were going to do it up really big tonight baby, but fate happens. I want a rain check, OK? Anyway, I know I'm about to run out of time (cough) and

(*You have 30 sec*)

I'm not supposed to be on the phone so listen up. The police officers are going to take you to the car and there are some things I want you to get out, very important things, baby I don't feel too good, good drugs I guess, but baby just know I love you girl and we'll talk tomorrow. And baby...... **Beeeeeeeeeeeeeeeeep**

Oh my goodness, was that my phone beeping like that? What was that?

Code stat, code stat...

"Hello, hello. We have to hang up now. The patient has gone into cardiac arrest! Someone will call you with his condition –beep – hello? Oh my, he was talking to an answering machine. Oh well, too late, he's gone – look, flat lined. He sure was determined to talk to her. It must be nice to be loved like that. Whatever she was busy doing cost him his last call. Talk about loving somebody 'til death.

What she'll never know is that in his car were two dozen, crushed from the accident, long stemmed American beauty red roses. In his glove compartment was the paperwork from the house closing, in addition to the travel itinerary for their seven day honeymoon trip to Barbados. And under his bible was a little burgundy box with an engagement ring that would make even the well-to-do raise an eyebrow. With the box was a poem he had written just for her. He'd had it professionally copied onto parchment paper in gold leaf calligraphy. This was to be the perfect proposal to his wife to be. He had indeed planned THE SWEETEST THING and it NEVER HAPPENED.

She arranged a graveside memorial service choosing long stemmed American Beauty red roses as the floral casket spray. Soft harp and violin music filled the air on this beautiful sun filled afternoon. As the casket was lowered into the ground, three dozen white doves were released racing toward the indigo sky into the fluffy, glorious white clouds. Slowly lifting her hand, she waved farewell to the spirit of her departed loved one. And speaking softly with a sigh she said "We'll meet again my love, bye-bye." Suddenly she glanced left, and on her shoulder, landing gently, a beautiful butterfly.

THE END

LOVING US
FIT FOR US
WOE IS US

I'VE ONLY HAD SALAD!

Ms Cynthia

I've only had salads
Since I left this place
You say "Impossible"
Girl, get out of my face!

I need to see the doctor
I'm so hungry, I'm pale
I need to ask him
Where'd he get this damn scale?

I know what I've eaten
I'm the one who was there
Girl, you're a size three
I don't expect you to care

Get his ass out here!
I need some answers now!
How'd I gain ten extra pounds?
He needs to tell me how?

Doc, I've been eating salads
Exactly like you said
I've even been eating one
before I go to bed

A little lettuce, tomato and cheese
A little ham, egg and blue cheese
Ranch dressing, olives and chives
Bacon bits and croutons; small size
Hell man, I'm trying to stay alive!

Some pasta salad and Cole slaw
A few chicken wings too
Potato salad and crackers,
Hey, I get hungry just like you
Some pineapple and apple rings
A few bowls of soup on the side
Cream of chicken, cream of broccoli
 two small yeast rolls. Well, I tried

They were out of diet coke
So, sweet tea to wash it down
To stay on my oatmeal intake
One, two raisin oatmeal cookies
While shopping in town

I've only eaten green salads,
What other color would I eat?
I'm following doctor's orders
I won't stand for failure or defeat

Sure sometimes I reward myself
But only a small decadent token
Forget what that skinny, wiener bitch said,
that doggone scale is broken!

I increased my cheese intake
extra calcium should be better
You said 3 servings of dairy
I had Colby jack, jalapeno and cheddar

featuring **Sister Lula Mae Davis:**

Hon, I know what you mean, same thing happened to me
Look, I'm sitting here big and round, just fluffy as I can be
I ate those salads just like you, sometimes two or three
I told the doc, just like you "No sir, this here can't be"
I guess them there salads just ain't for you and me
Let's go get us some lunch, hm-m- let me see….
A nice buffet with dessert, you know it, sweet iced tea
I'll be glad to go with you, but you know this ain't on me?
Well let's go – you drive

Remember, stop that cussin'
You know the Lord is listening
Oh, I know, you're still a **good** Christian

How Much Do You Care About Your HAIR DOWN THERE?

Ms Cynthia

How much do you care about your hair?
You know what hair; the hair down there
Did you know that hair needs extra care?

Do you shape, arch, trim or pick it?
Comb, brush, how do you fix it?
Do you curl, pluck, wash and shave it?
Shampoo, dry, gel and wave it?

Do you dye it, braid it and celebrate it?
Or trim it - grow it - then debate it?

Is it straight, bushy, curly or nappy?
Pleased, frustrated, frigid or happy?
Is it blond, brunette, red or brown?
Can't remember huh, haven't looked down?

Is it streaked, frosted or highlighted blond?
Surely you're having responsible fun!
Yes the 70's, long hair was hipper
Its 2000 girl, please get a hedge clipper!

I'll bet some have curly tresses
With little bows that match your dresses
Who out there ever tried to tweeze it?
Blow, brush it out and tease it?
And which conditioner will please it?

Ever tried the wax - Brazilian?
So many female products – a gazillion
Ladies just remember when horsing that motor
Be sure its fresh and there's not a foul odor

" *Who knows where the nose goes when the doors close*"

IS THE GYNO A Gigolo OR WHAT?

MS CYNTHIA

Tell me honestly, what other profession would fine-upstanding women wait for one man in a white jacket, sometimes for over an hour, and pay him good money to put on a purple rubber glove to play in all her private parts? We allow him to have his mistress-in-crime come in and tell us to get undressed, put on cheap paper lingerie, lay on a porn table as he instructs us to "scoot, scoot, scoot on down and spread 'em wide".

"Yeah, that's good, can you come down just a little more?"

"knees wide apart now",

while she looks on getting him all sorts of toys out of a drawer; cold toys at that, while you - feet in stirrups, wide open - absolutely no dignity, attempt to breathe through it all. "No, I'm fine"

And the real killer - he sits on a stool just below your womanhood placing his finger in places while pressing your lower tummy to make sure you feel his presence, "just a little pressure, how's that"?

He even tells you with a smirk, "This may be a little uncomfortable"

"just relax"

"You're doing good". They both take samples, slides and

pictures of secretions

to share with their friends, sending them off, to only God knows where, without your permission. You don't even sign a release form.

Of course, he's got other toys in his pockets and around his neck.

"Open wide, now breathe deeply for me."

"Let me see here, how's that? What about that? Can you feel this? He prods, pokes and sheds light on things your mate has never even seen. He's got all types of gels, creams, lotions and sprays just for

your comfort.

He stands over you while you lie there helpless. He caresses, lifts and separates your breast one at a time while watching you squirm when he places his K-Y'd finger in your anal cavity – **What??**

Then he sends his accomplice out so he can speak to you gently
while looking into your eyes.
"Are you ok? This was all for your good and everything looks great."
Then the lie; as on any date "I'll call you
with the results, that is, if necessary"
"Now take this to the lady behind the desk to set up your next session, oh,
I meant appointment".

And what do we do? "Yes sir, I'll wait for your call,
but can I call you?" "No, I'd rather you didn't,
I'll call you if there's a need. OK?"
OK, I'll just go pay now, oh, silly me, I already paid.
"Alrighty, see you next time. Everything looks good down there."

If that ain't running the best damn Gigolo game around

No hors devours, much less dinner for two
What's the white dinner jacket for?
No soft lights, candle lights or wine
at best, some 'muzac' from a musical movie score
(If you've got insurance)
And he's off to see his next woman in waiting
before you can get out the door.

Other women coming and lining up in droves
ready and willing to take off their panties
letting him see and play in it all

Cash and most insurance accepted
Please pay before service is rendered
There will be a fee for all cancellations
Thank you for your patronage

Dr. Gyno Gigolo
Just like a pimp
Both make money by keeping women naked;
and the women gotta pay
Only difference - one's legal
PLAY ON PLAYER

JUST US GIRLS- female anatomy

MS CYNTHIA

Hi, come on in, it's just us girls. Come meet my friends. We're really just like sisters, like family, you know. We all live in the same general area, but we hardly ever take time to get to know each other as we should. So we're just kind'a hanging out, as they say, "venting – no panties." We all could use a breather, I'm sure you understand. Let me introduce you to everyone.

First, this is my girl **Clitoris**. "Hi, you can call me Clit. You should know that all of them are jealous of me. I'm a hot little ball of fire! I believe in having fun. I sit high and proud, and I don't apologize for it. When I'm aroused, let's just say, I'm simply beautiful, a sight to behold. Without me, there would be no fun. Sure, like everybody else, I get the finger from time to time, but mostly, I get sweet long kisses – and I love it! When I'm relaxed, I'm as soft as a kitten. The problem is that whenever they're having fun, he brushes against me. He's always hitting on me but they think it's my fault. They need to understand that I live on top and he has to go by me to get to them. Damn! Can't we all just get along"?

Whatever girl. Hi, I'm **Genatalia**, call me Talia. I'm the one who holds this group together. Well, me and my girl **Vulva**. You see I have this split personality so I'm able to get along with them all. I can get them to open up and share or shut them up when I get ready. Vulva and I kinda' oversee; keep them under control. We work together because; as I'm sure you can see, these sisters need supervision".

Down here is where cranky **Labia** lives. "Hey girl, hell yeah I'm cranky. I catch the brunt of it. It gets so hot and sticky down here and she lets him get on my last nerve. It's in and out, in and out, up and down, in and out. Hell, what does he think these are – saloon doors? They're starting to hang uneven, it's a wonder they haven't fallen off. She needs to pick up some KY or WD40 or something. Yeah, or lickity split. Ha!

Meet **Areola**. She was the one who told me you were here. She sits on this mound so she can detect what's going on around here. She signals to the rest of us what's coming down the pipe. She and the owner of this fine structure are close, so Areola usually knows what's up. She can't visit though. We have this sort of inter-cum system going. If she's approached, she let's the rest of us know to be prepared.

"So Genatalia, are we going out are what? And what are you going to do about that hair?" Vulva that's just rude, OK? Anyway, before we were so rudely interrupted, as you can see, I'm into the retro look. Vulva wants it trimmed to one of those barely there looks or just leave a little on top. Next she'll want the Brazilian wax. I'm not trendy like that. You know, with this natural part, I'm thinking two French braids, whata'ya think? Clitoris chimed in "whatever floats your little man in the boat. Are we ready?"

We're waiting on **Gluteus, Ms Maximus**. She's always running behind. "Ms Booty luscious, with her big-round-self! Talk about being too much. Evidently not, **Minimus** supports her in all her

endeavors, even though he just stays under her ass. "Yeah, and sometimes, he can be so anal, a real a-hole."
He sticks so close to her, she can't fart unless he's there to smell it first hand. "Yeah, that's another thing, he smells funny". That's OK, she says she needs him. One thing we know for sure, she's always got our back. Besides, he looks up to her. "Looks up her?" No girl, up to her, whatever, here she comes dragging ass as usual.

So where are we hanging out? Well I thought the **G-spot,** but it's always so hard to get in there. Yeah but if we do, (they all say in unison) "Satisfaction Guaranteed!" I know, that G-spot is smoking like a crock pot. You know we have to pass right by The **Nappy Dugout**, we can run in there for a hot minute. "The Nappy Dugout, that hole in the wall? Well at least there are walls in that hole! Anyway **Vagina** has remodeled and everything. I heard that it's very plush inside now. She has all the hottest shades of baby pink, cotton candy and fuchsia. And now it's **Members Only**. She upgraded to first class, it's now "Vagina's Walls". "Well, I gotta see this for myself, because she used to let them tear that place up – it was awful."

I know but remember when we all were about fourteen, so firm, so innocent, well, maybe not so innocent, but innocent enough. The most we would get was a rub here, a rub there, you know - but Vagina, that girl was on lock down. She would peep through her screen door. She wouldn't come out and no one was allowed in. And just as soon as she blew out that last candle on her sixteenth birthday cake, POP went the weasel. That little weasel she gave it up to saw the blood from that cherry and it scared him shitless.

She never saw him again. Vagina felt rejected so the next thing we knew she had visitors all the time. That's when Labia showed up. Back then she didn't complain so much. "What the hell do you mean by that? OK, you try to handle in and out, in and out". That's why I'm still irritable to this day – I'm irritated! You don't know my pain!" Anyway, Vagina had more traffic than a freeway at five o'clock pm. That's why we called her 'Hole in the Wall'. Sometimes it felt like they were drilling holes in her walls, but she's a better woman now, she's damn near a lady. "Let's not get carried away. I wouldn't say she's a lady, just more discriminating and selective. She's still a hottie." Well, her previous behavior made us all look bad. "And smell bad too. It was a hot, funky mess down here. She was really placing all of us at risk. There was indeed a 'fungus among us'."Girls I know you recall some of those guys, oh my. "And the size of some of those guns they were packing, I tell you." "Hell yeah, I'll tell you too", said Labia, "in and out, in and damn out, wore me out!"

I'm sure that's why **Uterus** had to move. Vagina was having so many problems with those **Ovary twins**. Every time he dropped his boys off to swim, the twins would send little hot-ass messages out to meet them. Vagina knew they were going to make babies and drop them off on Uterus and she'd have a house full of kids. "I thought you said Vagina had security for that." She did, but you know you can't find good help these days. You can't trust them not to let them in. They had on rubber suits but they could still possibly slip by. "I know that's right, that's a job from the womb to the tomb." So Vagina told Uterus she would have to go but those little hot twins could stay. They really could be of help around here without Uterus around for them to run to.

What did you say your name was again? "Lou Brie".
Lou Brie as in **Lubrication**? I thought I recognized you girl, they call you Silky right? "Yeah, that's right". I remember Uterus talking about you, said you were slick. She was always saying she wished you would visit more often, and now she's gone. So where've you been until now, "I just got discharged, but I've been here before. I already knew Uterus left, that's why I'm here. I'm here to help with the O twins. Since Vagina has a new place she wanted everything nice and shiny with shimmering walls; that's what I do". Well girl, why didn't you say so. We can just slide on up in there. You've got inside connections. "Thank goodness" said Labia, "you and I are going to be best friends. You can make it easy on a sister around here Slick, Silky, whatever you go by – welcome."

Look girls, Vagina's new place is really nice! It looks so nice and clean. "It smells great in here too; fresh. It's nice but too narrow for me." That's what they like, it's cozy and plush. I never thought I would say that about this place, it's really classy. The colors are so warm and relaxing. Oh look up there, that's where Uterus used to live. Oh my, it looks dark up there. Yeah, I think that's the VEP room. "You mean the VIP don't you?" No, the VEP room for very endowed penises. She won't have to worry about too much traffic up there, that endowment has got to be large and in charge. "The fewer, the better I say." "Me too" said Labia.

Vagina's got security and full protection, she's ready.
Remember those funky milk drinks she used to serve? "No more of that girl. She only serves champagne now and no more cigars allowed. Remember those? What in the hell was she thinking?"

I don't know but they sure did stink. "I personally don't like champagne; it looks and taste like pee." Most of it probably is pee, but you know men don't care, they'll still cum here. They all laughed aloud. "Yeah, and some guys even prefer pee, remember?" O.K. ladies, be nice, this is a new day for all of us – a fresh start. I'm personally proud of Vagina.

Before Uterus moved out, she'd convinced Vagina that reds, once a month, would be a healthy alternative. Vagina really didn't care for the idea and no one seemed to be interested. In fact, everyone stayed away during that time. Vagina was just sick and cramped about it; no traffic at all.

Well ladies, to a fresh start. Let's toast to healthier more pleasurable days. And when we leave here let's head to the G-Spot. Hot Volcanoes and Screaming Orgasms for everyone – on me! Come on Clitoris, get us started girl. "You know me, that's what I was designed to do. And I'm proud to say, I do it so well! Here's to getting to know each other better and promising to work together as a team." They all exclaim in unison "As a team - we're awesome!"

GOOD BYE TO PIES
STAY AWAY FAT THIGHS

Ms Cynthia

She looked in the mirror and spoke to herself; all of herself.
She spoke personally to every lump, bump, and roll...

Hi Everyone,
We're all here to say good bye to our excess
We need not name names; you know who you are
You moved in gradually, never left, this is your verbal eviction
To be fair, you have ninety days and you're out-a-here.

Hello Jell-O
Hello arms that no longer have charm
We'll all look back and have a good laugh

Good bye thunder thigh
sweet round face, sweet as a pie
I'll get you in check, you three part neck
No more ease for you cottage cheese flabby knees

Smaller, at least you might stand a bit
My sad, hanging flabby tits
Oh yeah you – you know what
It's over Ms Buttercup butt
We've got to get moving!

I'm sick and tired of cries
from sweaty, rubbing thighs
I need healthful tips for these oversized hips
And it's a must
I lift and separate my bust

What I'm serving up now, you won't want a bite
Great! Bite off some of this cellulite!

Tomatoes, spinach and lots of celery
Like it or not – that's how it's gonna be
Ah yes beets; I'll be back in pleats
Fresh veggies and lots of greens
Proud to get back in trendy jeans

That's not all I've got in store
Listen up, I've got much more
Kool aid and sodas – don't even bother
Girls we're drinking clean, clear water, water, water

No white rice, meat with smothered gravy
Looking like I'm having a baby
We will have a little brown rice
Whole grain carbs; that'll be nice

No more fudge
can't get it to budge
Maybe a little red wine sometime
Antioxidants, I know, a little will be fine

We ate whenever you wanted to
cake, fries, grease, even fondue
We sipped, drank and slurped, Cappuccino-ed too
That's over now and so are you

Bidding farewell, once and for all
Don't even think about it, don't come back or call
I'm getting healthy, getting fit
I'm really sick and tired of this sh-t
flushing all of it out of my life
I'll be a healthy mom, friend and sexy wife

Now let's take a picture; all of you and me
I'll remember how to feed my family
Gonna look good, too good to be true
Oh, and when you leave
could you take these fat clothes with you?

Please? Really I won't be in need of them.
Maybe you can use them where you're going.
Remember you're not welcome back here!

THAT'S THE LAST WORD – PERIOD!

MS CYNTHIA

Promise: I won't complain and say you cramp my style
I'll relax, we'll have tea - and I'll even smile
I'll even get spruced up and take you out
We'll have fun, dance, scream and shout
But I really need to see you – like right now!
When you show up I'll curtsy and even bow

Come on, stop playing, I really do care
Where the hell are you? I can't find you anywhere
Not on the back of my expensive white skirt
In case you showed up, I wore a long shirt
Not in my favorite satin arm chair
Not in my Vicky's lace underwear

I won't talk bad about you to my friends
How long is this sentence? When will it end?
So, so sorry I took you for granted
Please tell me a seed is not planted

It's been two or three days, I'm counting the hours
Please come to me, let's take a warm shower
Aaaaah, oooooh that's nice, I'm relaxed

There you are! Don't ever do that again!
And by the way, where in the hell have you been?
Tell me where'd you go?
Way past time for you to show
Stop hiding under exclamations and question marks
You want literature? Come quickly – hark!
Every 28 days I want you here!
I need to see you every month of every year -PERIOD!
I'm really glad to see you... That was so- not funny ha-ha...
You play entirely too much,
grow up would ya?

FROM PAMPERS TO DEPENDS
DRIP, drip, drip

MS CYNTHIA

Whack on the bottom
tears drip, drip drip
first teeth, learning to eat
drool drip, drip
School days, cold days
coat, hat, glove days
nose holes drip, drip, drip

Cute teenage girl now
Almost a woman now
What's a period now?
menstrual drip, drip, drips

Dates, proms, high school graduation
Boys, peer pressure, parent's frustration
Results in underarm perspiration
drip, drip, drip

First job, college education
forehead drip, drips
Before the alter; married sensation
tears drip, drip
Wedding night hesitation
Love making penetration
Passion filled vibrations
drip, drip, drip

Baby's coming; water breaks
drip, drip, drip
baby needs healthy milk
breast drip, drip

Finally menopausal – no more drips
Oh no – hot flashes – drip, drip, drip
Water running down my face
What else is there to face?
Down my leg into my shoe
That's what incontinence will do
From pampers to depends, women
drip,
    drip,
        drip

FRIEND GIRLS RECIPE

MS CYNTHIA

This recipe is sure to win over your girlfriends as well as teach them a lesson or two about what a true girlfriend will do or go through just for you.

12 long stemmed "I thank you girl"
3 bunches of fresh, fragrant hugs "we all make mistakes, its ok"
2 level-headed "I really appreciate you" statements
½ cup of low calorie powdered sugar coating (don't over do, keep it true)
2 cups of warm tea and honey with lemon "Tell me more girl" or "Sugar you know you can call me anytime of the day or night, even weekends"
Pour on the compliments and uplifting comments. "That outfit compliments you"
Fold in encouraging observations. "Your presentation covered all points – great job!"
Toss in a few heaping spoonfuls of "I love you no matter what"
Blend in fresh colorful seasonal flowers just because "They reminded me of your smile"
2 bottles of your newly discovered wine and two nice wine glasses (one bottle for the two of you to share and the other for…well… you know)
Wrap firmly in a "Congratulations girl, I knew you could do it!"

This recipe goes extremely well with and are actually complimented by 2 bowls of Rocky Road or Heavenly Hash ice cream
Followed by 2 cups of freshly brewed coffee or cappuccino in hand painted china cups. Loads of whipped cream – mandatory!

For the weight conscious divas – 1 package of chocolate thin mints and a bottle of raspberry flavored, no calorie sparkling water in crystal wine glasses. or splurge…

2 chilled, sugar rimmed wine goblets with freshly washed red seedless grapes (White grapes may cause gas; let's not ruin the festive mood)
1 bowl of your most decadent white and dark chocolates
1 bowl of fresh red ripe strawberries (as stated before – whipped cream is mandatory)
1 plate of fresh sliced golden pineapple or ripe peaches or both
1 variety cheese tray – crackers, bread optional
a bottle of your favorite sparkling dessert wine or expensive champagne

Partner these with easy listening music, scented candles and lots of laughs.
The next morning will be a breeze (after all of that fruit). Just smile and be free, say excuse me and remember this recipe

A PERFECT RECIPE FOR GIRLFRIENDSHIP

SOUTHERN SWEETNESS

MS CYNTHIA

Sugar britches, for your darling baby doll
Try sugar plums and a nice golden honey bun
Then, Sweet Cakes, taste the syrupy butter cup
from the tulips while sipping a mint julep
Pout your soft luscious lips, sniff a whiff…yum
Now Honey, suckle that sweet tater pie
Now wasn't that nice Nanna Puddin?
Feel the breeze from the soft plush pussy willow?
More velvety than a red velvet cake
Icing too sweet? Need some water Melon ?
Sugar Daddy, that candy cane ran circles
up, down and around that cherry pie
Was that cherry tart? Filling warm and gooey?
That passion flower fruit is edible; *a may pop*
It *may pop-* may not
Ever see the fire fly from a dragon fly Butterfly?
Sh-h-h, hu-ush puppy or no buttered molasses
for your hot corn balls
Listen, Honey Child, you'll get a bunch a' nectar
from your finger lick'n moist apple dumpling

Shoot yeah, Sugar babe will be your creamy sweetie pie
Oh my! Is honeydew?
Now ya'll love bugs cantaloupe!
Just marry up with tangerine and nectarine
That'll just be peachy keen as ice cream
Fine as muscadine wine; gimme mine
Now go on and have a good time Cupcakes
Them two are simply sweet as frosting drizzle
Let me lick that spoon!

I don't know what got into me. I was raised better than that.
Just so I don't shame pure Southern Sweetness
try this next one on for size – Let's just say
it's a little more digestible…

PURE SOUTHERN HOSPITALITY

Ms Cynthia

This is suppose to be about hospitality
Certainly not sexuality
But guess what - **we've got that too!**

If you came a look'n for hot links **Hot Cakes**
sweet cakes, sweet milk
butter milk, butter beans
sweet bread, cornbread
buttered bread or buttered biscuits
We've got that too!

You want sweet tea **Sweet Pea?**
Kool -Aid red? That's what I said
Red's not only a color, it's a flavor
Don't believe me? – Well, ask my neighbor!
I ain't kiddin – Shut your mouth
That's how we do it in the south
Just have a deep dish cobbler good time
We've got that too!

What's all that fuss you make?
When we say 'a hoe', it's a hoe cake
Careful now, don't step on the critters
Be real nice - we'll fry you corn fritters
Hush puppy – it ain't hard on your figure

Ya'll come back ya hear
Make it real soon (Like when the cow jumps over the moon)
No sir-ree , I ain't being mean
Especially if your money is collard green
Are ya'll leaving? Safe bye –bye
May your trip be as smooth as a Mississippi mud pie
And we've got that too!

GETTIN FIT

MS CYNTHIA

Pam: Yes girl, this year I'm gettin fit
All of this weight, I'm tired of it
Gonna work hard, not gonna quit
By this summer, I'll be the sh-t!

Keisha: Me too girl, gotta get my body tight
Gonna work hard; day and night
No not that; not this time
I'll be so fine, it'll be a crime
Bet all your pennies on this dime

Helena: I'm committed; I'm getting it off
I'm going to be fine, no matter the cost
Gonna shake and shake 'til I shake it away
Back in my bikini in a month and a day

Group: *Hey Sister Davis, since you're always giving us good advice, based on all that wisdom you've built up, how about joining us in our weight loss mission. You can pray for us when we get slack. Come on, join the team!*

Sis Lula Mae Davis: Girls, I'm way too old to get it back right
Ain't no way to get this body back tight
If I exercise all day and pray all night
If I pray to the sister angels with all my might
But thank you girls for asking - let me pray on it.

(*Lord knows they need the Spirit of Jesus in their midst, I'd better* **be there for 'em. Bless their little heathen hearts, they need me**)

One month and a day later

Pam: Girl, I've been struggling for thirty days
 I've been stretching and bending all kind of ways.
 Read **Shape, In Shape, Out of shape** magazines
 I'm aching and sore as hell - still can't get in my jeans
 All these sit-ups, my stomach is swollen round
 Damn, if I didn't gain an extra four pounds
 Eight glasses of water? Yeah right, water weight
 While holding this water weight, no need to fake
 Give me a slice of that chocolate cake

Keisha: I know girl, same thing happened to me
 Watched **In Style** and **Out Of Style** on my TV
 Ordered gym wear, skin care, footwear, hair care
 Bought wristbands, sweatbands even gloves for my hands
 a step-o-meter and the latest in home machines
 Thirty days later and I ain't lost a damn thing!
 Counting carbs, counting steps
 Look, here's the journal I kept
 I tried I promise, did all I can
 I burned more calories sleeping with my man

Helena: I danced it off, walked it off, even tried to talk if off
 I tossed it, flossed it, even tried to salsa it off,

                Metamucil-ed, prune juiced and peed it off
                Stretched and pilat-ed and green tea-ed it off
                Made a deal I could feel, Jack and Jilled it off
                It was so good I think I squealed it off
                Don't dismiss me with a smile or frown
                I'm feeling good and I'm down three pounds

Group: Well Sister Davis, did you pray yours away?

Sister Davis: Well I started by asking – "Lord help me please"
                And right away the pain left my aching knees
                Next thing the pain left from my lower back
                I talked to the Lord while walking on the track
                Got up early and walked every morn
                I tell you, Sister Davis feels reborn
                In my yard, messed around and got a splinter
                So I worked out at the senior center
                In elasticized pants, I jubilantly raised my hands
                And God bless, I messed around and found me a man
                Anyhow, he works out to exercise his heart
                He must drink lot'sa prune juice; he's apt to fart
                Awh, ain't nothing wrong wit that, he's only human
                You girls will laugh at anything, acting like clowns
                Sweat on this little girls, Sister Davis lost ten pounds
                I actually gained 150lbs if you count Mr. Henderson.
                I got the last laugh again, tee-hee-hee

FREE YOUR GIRLS!

WRITTEN BY MS CYNTHIA

"TAKE 'EM OUT, TAKE 'EM OUT!"
"LET 'EM SCREAM. LET 'EM SHOUT!"
"LET 'EM OUT, LET 'EM OUT!"
"NEED A BREAK, AIR 'EM OUT!

HONEY, TURN THOSE GIRLS A LOSE
SEEMS YOU'VE GOT 'EM IN A NOOSE
BEFRIEND YOUR GIRLS, CALL A TRUCE
HYDRATE YOUR GIRLS, DRINK SOME JUICE!

SICK AND TIRED OF STAYING IN
NEED TO BREATHE, THEY NEED TO BEND
IN CONSTANT BONDAGE, AIN'T THAT A SIN?
THOSE GIRLS HAVE ISSUES TO DEFEND

THEY WANT TO PUT ON SOMETHING SILKY
FEEL SEXY, FULL AND MILKY
NOT FLANNEL OR RAYON; TIRED, 'ILKY

SWINGING FREE; TO AND FRO
FREEDOM, REVOLUTION, A SONG - YOU KNOW?
LET 'EM DANCE, BOUNCE AND SMILE
JIGGLE AND JUMP AROUND BUCK WILD
POINT FOLKS OUT - LAUGH AND HOWL

NOW, IS THIS TOO MUCH TO ASK?
NOT TO WORRY, A SIMPLE TASK
IN THE SUN? LET THEM BASK
TOO ASHAMED? HERE'S A MASK!

TURN 'EM LOOSE AT LEAST ONE NIGHT
FEE L 'EM UP, THEY'RE YOURS ALRIGHT
RELAX 'EM BEFORE THAT MAMMOGRAM BITE
BUST- FULL, BUST-FALLEN, SILICONE OR BUST-LITE

Lefty's Story

MS CYNTHIA

OK, I think I'm ready to vent my feelings now. I just need to lay it out there. You know this is so difficult for me to talk about. She and I were always together. I mean, since we were little, when you saw one you saw the other. We grew up together, saw and experienced things together. We got our first bra at the same time and talked about how we were growing and getting bigger together.

After we became teens, sure, one received more attention than the other but that's to be expected. We were still inseparable, a great two-some "For life!" we vowed. When I hurt, it's like she could feel my pain and like-wise, I hers. It's like we were twins or something. We understood each other that way.

I'll never forget that dreadful day we both went to get our annual physical, everything seemed fine, neither of us had any complaints. It was the usual touch, squeeze, feel. We actually talked about that part being kind of a turn on, and then the big mama, that damned woman crusher, the mammogram machine. After the brutal nipple buster and the usual "we'll call you", we both laughed and thought, yeah, that's what our last date said.

Then the call, the come in, I couldn't let her go by herself, so of course, I tagged along. After all we were closer than sisters.
The office visit with the doctor left us both more crushed than that titty crusher ever could have. The news, the terror and the tears that I was about to lose my closest friend forever was overwhelming. To think, I would be recognized as a survivor after having lost an actual part of myself.

Yes, I'm Lefty, but she left me and I'm here today because I wasn't the right one. My neck said, "Well, look at me, I just hang around by myself all the time. I just try to keep my head up and not worry that people always try to hang things on me. It starts to have a choking effect after awhile." My navel was no comfort. "You know me, I just stay in and curl up most of the time. I'm considered an introvert you know." The arms said, "At times I feel that my partner and I are miles apart. Sometimes we do things together, but you know what they say *-don't let your right hand know what you left hand is wearing,* funny, ha, ha?"

I'm Lefty and I feel left out, like a left over, left behind. Hell, even the behind gets more action than I do. I feel hung over and I sure could use a lift or a pick-me-up. I still have feelings and I'd like to feel appreciated even though she's gone. It's like I'm invisible or something. I need attention more now than ever. Don't neglect me; don't make me regret I'm still here. I know I'm a constant reminder of when she was here, when things were fine, but she's gone OK? Either get me another partner or learn to love me for me, and let somebody else love me too. Don't hide me away as if I don't exist. Did you ever think or consider how that makes me feel? Remember, I'm the left one, the one with the heart, I need love. Yes, I'm Lefty and there's still a lot left to me. Thanks for letting me get that off my chest. **HELLO,** what does a girl have to do to be valued around here? Maybe I should tell Victoria my secret.

WE GIRLS
&
OUR ISSUES

DAMAGED GOODS

Written by Ms Cynthia

HIM: "Hello, may I buy you a drink?
      Would you care to dance?
      I noticed you standing over here
      Overwhelmed with just one glance
      Why are you here all alone?
      Perhaps I could call you on the phone
      Maybe one day, you'll allow me to escort you home"

HER: "Oh yeah, sure, I know your type
      Sharp, clean-cut, full of hype
           Yeah, you think I look just ripe
           hot enough to smoke in your pipe
           In bed you think you're dy-no-mite!
      Yeah, OK, so what you're fine
      you get girls panties every time –
      believe me, you won't get mine
           You thought that, didn't you? I'm sure you did
           I'll bet you won't even like my kid
      You'll rip out my heart, and not even call
      Then tell me you were playing basketball
           You'll come late at night and come-a-cuma-cuma
           Next day it's your baby-mama-drama
              No deal, no way, too cute for that
              I'm a tall, slim honey; all muscle, no fat
      I work, I'm smart, and a reader too
      I'm not about to fall for a playa' like you

        Oh yes, I'm sure we've met before
          You're every guy that's ever been to my door
    And I'm not going for it anymore
    No, no more and that's for sure!"

HIM: "Ooo-K, never miiiind, sorry to have bothered you."
      He backs away with the utmost caution.

Little china doll on the shelf
So, so pretty all by herself
Moved too fast, far too soon
Cancelled dreams sing a salty tune

She's been used time and again
Left sitting pretty trying to pretend
Doesn't need love- love doesn't miss her
Perhaps bitter for life, back away kind sir
Sorry, her pussycat forgot how to purr

YES! I SHOP 'TIL I DROP

Ms Cynthia

Who came up with shop 'til you drop?
I guess it's my fault; but clearly, I need rehab

Clothes and trinkets everywhere, cause I shop 'til I drop
Absolutely no time to spare, cause I shop 'til I drop
Seven sets of dinner ware
Dishes now are everywhere
Dishes, glasses and silverware
I can't find a matching pair
Shop for more? Do I dare?
I shop 'til I pop and I'm about to drop

Boots, pumps all types of shoes – I shop 'til I drop
Bras, panties, disposable boobs - I really need to stop
Skirts, pants, tops and dresses
Jackets, blouses and sweater vest-es
Socks, hair bows and Panty hose
The money I spend; nobody knows
I'm overwhelmed from my head to my toes
'Cause I shop 'til I drop, I know I need to stop

Can someone help me please?
Here someone take my keys
They're having this great white sale
Sent a reminder in the mail
Do I need more sheets? I can't tell
I'll shop 'til I drop

I'm ready to confess; I can't handle this stress
My house is a total mess. The stores are winning, it's no contest
– I shop 'til I drop!

I do it at the grocery store
I have enough - still buy more
I pay with checks, cards and cash
To the mall, a mad dash
Parking; trying not to crash
I need help really fast
So I don't shop 'til I drop, can't someone help me stop?

PUT IT ON MY CARD

MS CYNTHIA

Great buy on shoes! Put it on my card
Good music, jazz and blues – Put it on my card
Here you are, on my college loan
I forgot to pay on my phone
Yes I'd like the new ring tone
Just put it on my card

I've simply got to have that dress,
Look at this hair, it's such a mess
Gotta get my script for this stress
Here, just put it on my card

To the ATM to get some cash
Gum, bottled water, chips and gas
Utilities, car insurance, cable bill's past
New perfume, makeup, OK that's the last
I'm putting it all on this card

"What do you mean, I need to pay?
You know good and well it's not payday!
Would you please stop calling me?
Yes I did, I paid the minimal fee
I'm trying to pay you, it's really hard
Why did you mail me this damn card?

Yes, I'll make arrangement. I'll really try
You'll hear from me soon, OK, yes, bye
Treating me like they're the credit guard
All because of this plastic-ass card!

Girls, after work let's meet for drinks
All this pressure, hell, I can't think
Like I'm rocking ice and wearing mink
Threatening my credit down the sink

"Have fun girls, I've got these drinks
Yes, just put it on my card…
OK try this one…
Well, what about this one…
There must be some mistake
Sorry try this one…

NO MORE ROOM IN MY MENTAL WOMB

Ms Cynthia

The other day I was speaking with a male associate of mine. We had spoken on many occasions about doing something creative and he was phoning to see if I had come up with any ideas. Already overwhelmed, I immediately said to him "Please, my mind is pregnant with more than sextuplets right now and I can't even fathom another embryonic concept. You come up with something and I'll gladly provide cerebral milk to feed the infant idea until maturation. But honey, my mental womb simply cannot accommodate another single fertilized design or fetal initiative right now. I'm already sitting on a few eggs waiting for them to hatch, I've got irons in the fire; too hot to handle, droppings from that bird in the hand while still watching those two in the bush, pondering whether to **"Let's Make a Deal"** or **"come on down, The Price is Right"**.

I'm actually wondering if I'm **Smarter than a Fifth Grader**. Sometimes I think I'm **the Negotiator** or, tell me, do I have a stamp on my forehead that screams **"Lean on me"**? Not!

He calmly said, in his eloquent baritone voice "OK, I'll see what I can come with". I said to him, in amazement, "so you understood what I just said?" He said "of course, it was quite clear though very colorful, but Yes, I understood exactly what you were saying". I calmed down and said to him – "*oh*".

And that's why I love the creative minds of people in the Arts – they get it. Thanks **power-poet**, I'm so thankful you write.

THE MALL IS EVIL

MS CYNTHIA

Ladies think – why go to the mall?
Knowing everything is two sizes too small
Frustrated, aggravated trying to shop
Need a treat? There's the Dip & Dot

Headed out, trying to get home
"Ma'am, need a better offer on your cell phone?"
Overwhelmed by it all, answers or a tip
What's up with these cookies? Huge chocolate chip

You run past the sale signs, run past the bling
Turn the corner and there's the smell of wings
You know its evil – their acts are lewd
They've got an entire court of food

Displays, lights, mark ups to mark down
You're out of cash? Honey, put your card down
Can't fit the clothes, soon a mental rut
Close to the door – "Sale on hair cuts"

A bad choice, "why did I cut my hair?"
Looks awful; my hair is barely there
To top it off, I don't have a thing to wear

Ads in the daily news; oh my, a sale!
Triggers you back to the mall
Oh what the hell!

You cuss, swear, scream and shout
"I hate the damn mall"
Can't get it out of your mouth
A store knows when to call
Postcards and circulars
arrive in your monthly bill
I'm trying to tell you girls
The mall is evil!!!!

WHAT DA'YA MEAN WE'RE BREAKIN UP?

MS CYNTHIA

Hello, hello, what did you say? Surely, I mis-underheard you I could swear you said we were breaking up!

Now listen, I don't know what your problem is. Why, just this morning you talked about how well things were going, now you call me out of the blue and say something like this? **Who is she?**

OK, maybe I've been extra chatty lately, but all you had to do was say something. Oh, I guess I didn't let you get a word in huh? **Well, say something!** I've been a little slack but I was actually going out to purchase something cute to sleep in. I know you're sick of those same old tee shirts - your tee shirts. If it's the fast food three nights a week, I've also made plans to cook a little more so you're not cooking for yourself all the time. Also, my gynecologist says I'm fine now and we can resume sexual activities. I just can't believe you're fed up to the point of breaking up.

Ring tone

Hold on for a sec— *who in the hell could this be at a time like this?* Hello. How can you be calling me and I'm on the phone talking to you? Oh, the call was dropped. All I heard you say was… *we're breaking up, Oh, you meant the call was dropping…*

Oh baby, I love you so much and starting today I'm going to do all I can to let you know.

What do you mean what brought all of this on? Nothing baby – I just love you – that's all.

Still Sassy and Sexy at Seventy

Ms Cynthia

If you've ever wondered how I've come to grasp so much wisdom, it's because I make good use of the garden; the garden of wisdom. The garden of wisdom is filled with ladies that have lived this life and have experiences to share you wouldn't believe. I know if I take the time to listen to them talk about their husband, grown children and church, I'll eventually get the goods – the good and naughty.

This is a true story from one of my sister friends, a widowed vintage diva. This sister is now seventy three (73) years young and so full of life and vitality. She is my she-roe. She's active and community involved. Her sassiness is how you're suppose to grow, not old, but older. Anyway, check out her story. (Let us not judge)

She was out with some of her younger friend girls visiting one of the neighborhood bars. A nice looking gentleman came over and started to talk with one of the ladies. He knew her and she introduced him to everyone at the table. Most of these women were in their fifties or so. When he met my friend, she said he had an extra twinkle in his eye. Mind you, she is not your typical seventy something, you really need to see her to believe her appearance.

After some appetizers and cocktails the ladies were prepared to leave and he asked my friend to stay and continue to chat with him. She's always told me "always drive yourself and never allow someone else to be in charge of when you leave or where you go."

So needless to say, she stayed and continued to chat with the gentleman.

She said she told him up front, "you seem to be a nice fellow, but I'll just tell you, I'm far too old for you, how old are you anyway? The man said he was fifty two. She smiled and told him "see I told you, I'm almost ten years older than you are, I'm almost sixty two . He smiled and told her that she sure didn't look like it and he would like to spend some time with her, so they made a date. She said she dated him a couple of times and eventually she allowed him to come to her home – smart dating young divas. She said he was such a gentleman and called her often, she was starting to feel the urge. She allowed him to come back later in the week and the mood was set. To make a long story short- while making love, she said he whispered to her "baby, it's so hard to believe you're almost sixty two years old" which she replied "I know, it's hard for me to believe it sometimes myself." We laughed until we both cried and guess what – They're still dating!

I asked her "Girl are you practicing safe sex?" She told me "hell yeah, as hot as I am, I might still be able to conceive". We laughed aloud again until the tears streamed.
You know who you are and "You Go Diva – Sassy & Sexy at Seventy"

WHERE, OH WHERE ARE THE REAL MEN?

Ms Cynthia

(Now girls, you've got to put some neck action into this one)

Yes girl, I'm going out tonight
Sure enough I'm looking out' a sight!
Three tracks of weave sown in tight
Lashes long enough to distort my sight
These blue contacts will attract the light
Five inch stilettos for calves that's right!

Padded panties for that just right butt
Hair weave styled in that just right cut
'Wonder Bra' keeps the girls standing nice
Cleavage melting his cup of ice

Acrylic nails to rub over his back
Strutting spandex; a walking heart attack
Fake Louis Vuitton for my overnight pack
Imitation crab for my overnight snack

Fake designer cologne in my bag
My cousin's customized Jag
I'm looking good girl, like in the mags
I ain't no fakin, forsaken designer hag

Gonna fake it til I make it, whenever I can
Straight through stop signs waving my hand
Hitting all the clubs; a liar I can't stand
Got my radar on, scanning over this land
Looking, searching, scoping - trying to find a real man !

Female Vanity Stages

Ms Cynthia

BABY GIRL STAGE – Powder Pink & White

Snap t-shirts   fluffy blankets   extra absorbent Pampers
Lace up shoes   frilly socks   latest edition car seat
Baby powder   catnip tea   Mommy milk
pastel flannel gowns/booties   teething gel
                                               Apple juice

GIRL STAGE – Cotton Candy Pink

Dainty dresses   patent leather shoes   flowered panties
Bright colored tights ballet shoes   shiny new bike
Hair bows, ribbons   animal pajamas   whole milk
bubblegum spritz   kiwi tea   orange juice

TEEN STAGE – Hot Pink

Spandex jeans   wedge hill shoes   Kotex mini pads
Nike sneakers   matching bra & panties cool skate board
Lip gloss, mascara   spaghetti strap pajamas braces
Fruity body sprays   bottled lemon tea   chocolate milk,
                                                 fruit drink

DIVA STAGE - Fuchsia

Push up bras   sexy sandals   extra absorbent
                                                 Tampons
Stiletto high heels   French nail tips / highlites   Hot convertible
Victoria's Secret   diamonds & platinum   Kaluah & milk
Dolce & Gabbana   Long Island Iced tea   teeth whitening gel
                                               Champagne/O.J.

WOMAN STAGE- Mauve

Designer suits	long waist bras	panty liners
Sensible pumps	control top panties	Mercedes
Chanel #5	permanent hair color	soy milk
Oil of Olay	T-shirt sleepers	Bridge work, crowns
	Dieter's Tea	Cranberry juice

WISDOM STAGE - Rose

Sears, JC Penny wear		extra absorbent Depends
Hair pins/hair nets	talcum powder	senior activity bus
white bloomers	orthopedic shoes	Milk of Magnesia
Ponds cold cream	arthritis cream	dental cup/ Fixodent
Return to pastel flannel gown & booties		chamomile tea & prune juice

"TO PINK OR NOT TOO PINK'
ONLY A SHADE FROM BABIES TO LADIES
WE'RE ON LIFE 'S STAGE -
Have a Great Journey

PICTURES AND SHARED THOUGHTS FROM MY READERS

PICTURES

PICTURES COMMENTS

Comments

ABOUT THE AUTHOR

Ms Cynthia was born in and presently resides in Greenville, SC. This is her second published work of lyrical storytelling. She is also completing her, soon-to-be released CD, which features a collection of her writings, from both books, accompanied by the musical sounds and vocals of Wes McKelvey of **"Perfect Fitt"**

Ms Cynthia's Poetry/Jazz – "Love, Lies & Hanky Panky"

Ms Cynthia is also a motivational public speaker. She inspires and encourages, both male and female groups, with her openness yet respectful candor.

For readings or speaking engagements, contact her business manager, Napoleon Curtain - <u>NapCurtain@Yahoo.com</u>

Trained in Therapeutic Support Services and Crisis Intervention, Ms Cynthia incorporates those methods into her day to day dealings. Treating people with respect and speaking to them with understanding, love and non-judgment, is what she feels, encourages individuals to share their experiences with her. Writing those shared thoughts, opinions and circumstances, in a creative manner, help mask their identity, while it opens conversations, concerning women, we sometimes hesitate to speak candidly about.

Ms Cynthia feels - When women are healed, the children will flourish, and our future can and will be salvaged. She often reflects on her students from **New Foundations Family and Children's**

Services and **Connie Maxwell Children's Home,** for strength and inspiration to push for stronger women and mothers.

Ms Cynthia continues to work with mothers and their teenage daughters. She is presently working with **"Sisters Saving Sisters",** an organization that works with teen girls who would otherwise fall through the cracks of society. "Again, what the girls bring to the table is as rewarding as what the adult mentors offer to them. We continue to learn from each other as we grow toward greatness."

Ms Cynthia welcomes your comments and you are encouraged to write to her. tomscynthia@gmail.com